MARTYN WILLIAMS was born in Pontypridd in 1975. One of the leading rugby players in Wales for the past decade, he is hugely respected both on and off the field. After making his name with his home-town club, winning his first cap in 1996, he moved to Cardiff in 1999. Martyn has captained both Cardiff and Wales and been on two tours with the British Lions. In 2005, he was voted player of the Six Nations championship after taking a key role in Wales' Grand Slam triumph. Three years later he came out of international retirement to star in a second slam. Martyn lives on the outskirts of Cardiff with his wife and two children.

SIMON THOMAS has worked as a journalist in south Wales since 1989, specialising in covering rugby for the last thirteen years. After spending the best part of a decade with the South Wales Echo, he moved on to the national newspaper of Wales, the Western Mail, where he is currently employed as the paper's rugby correspondent. Simon lives in Cardiff with his wife and two children.

# martyn
# Williams
## the magnificent seven
### the autobiography

Martyn Williams with Simon Thomas

JOHN BLAKE

Published by John Blake Publishing Ltd,
3 Bramber Court, 2 Bramber Road,
London W14 9PB, England

www.johnblakepublishing.co.uk

First published in paperback in 2009

ISBN 978 1 84454 692 3

British Library Cataloguing-in-Publication Data:
A catalogue record for this book is available from the British Library.

Design by www.envydesign.co.uk

Printed in Great Britain by CPI Bookmarque, Croydon, CR0 4TD

3 5 7 9 10 8 6 4

Papers used by John Blake Publishing are natural, recyclable products made
from wood grown in sustainable forests. The manufacturing processes
conform to the environmental regulations of the country of origin.

To my wife, Sam, and our pride and joys
Mia and Corey, and to the memory of my mother,
Julie, and my brother, Craig.

# foreword
## by Steve Hansen

In the early days after I took over as Wales coach, I think Martyn – or Ginge as I know him – may have thought I was an absolute so-and-so, to put it mildly. But, in the end, I think he started to understand what I was about. There were times when I didn't play him and I know he was really disappointed. But these decisions were about looking after him and trying to lengthen his career, because he wasn't a big man.

Early on, I thought Martyn found things difficult because of his physical stature. But the Wales conditioning coaches Andrew Hore and Mark Bennett helped him produce more consistent performances, as his body became able to take the punishment that he put it through playing in such an involved position.

Ginge was a young man who desperately wanted Wales to be good and he wanted to be good himself. Probably, early on, he wasn't sure how he could do that. But he was willing and able to change certain things and he was always the first to try something new. First and foremost, his priority was the team. Martyn cared about the other guys. At times we wanted him to be the captain, but it wasn't something that sat easy on his shoulders. He would rather be a doer than an actual captain. In the end he became one of the leaders within the team. He became one of the main lieutenants and provided great support for his captain, which was role he was born for. It's the one he liked doing and it suited his game as well.

While Martyn's not a big man, he's certainly got a big heart and he plays true to it. He also plays with a lot of skill and he's a tremendous servant of Welsh rugby.
I enjoyed being around him, I enjoyed coaching him and I enjoyed his humour. It was a privilege to coach him and it remains a privilege to watch him play.

# acknowledgements

I would like to thank the following for their help and support in the preparation of this book:

My wife Sam for her patience, encouragement and all those long hours of child care; my stepdad Paul for everything he's done over the years and especially for those meticulously maintained scrapbooks which have been a priceless source of information; all the rest of my and Sam's family without whom none of this would have been possible; John Blake Publishing for giving me the opportunity to tell my story and particularly Clive Hebard and Michelle Signore for their work on this book; Mark Spoors and Louise Hewitt at Big Red Management; Huw Evans for all the great photos; Cardiff RFC historian Alan Evans, Pontypridd RFC and Cardiff Blues for help in compiling my career stats; Wales team manager Alan Phillips for his invaluable advice; all the great players I've been privileged to play with and against during my career; and last but not least my co-author Simon Thomas of the *Western Mail*, for helping to turn around this book in record time.

# contents

# introduction

# the seven rides again

Even if I'd scripted it myself, my return to international rugby couldn't have been any more perfect. It was a decision that could have backfired on me badly, because there's an old saying in sport that you should never go back. But, as it turned out, it proved to be one of the best calls of my life, as it brought me a second Six Nations Grand Slam and a series of personal landmarks along the way.

I had announced that I was quitting Test rugby the day after Wales were knocked out of the 2007 Rugby World Cup, but in truth I'd made the decision some time before that. Ever since going on the British Lions tour of New Zealand in 2005, I'd been finding it increasingly difficult to juggle all the different aspects of my life, what with my day job with the Cardiff Blues, international rugby, my family and trying to lay the foundations for a future career in the financial industry.

In particular, I was very aware of the amount of time I

was spending away from my family. I've got two children - my six-year-old daughter Mia and my son, Corey Craig, who is just under three. With me spending so much time away with Wales, it was putting a big burden on my wife, Sam. She has always been amazing and so supportive and I thought it was just fair that I should be around a lot more.

I also wasn't getting any younger so, at 32, I made the decision that the World Cup in the autumn of 2007 was going to be the end of the international line for me. Unfortunately it wasn't the swan song I had been hoping for, as we crashed out at the group stage with a shock defeat to Fiji.

Yet I'd made my mind up and there was no turning back – and for the first few weeks I was content that I'd made the right decision. But, gradually, the doubts started to creep into my mind.

It was when I went to watch Wales' first match after the World Cup, against South Africa at the Millennium Stadium, that I really first began to question what I had done. Myself and Wales' World Cup captain Gareth Thomas had been invited to go down to watch the game by Prince William, whose cup the teams were playing for. We had met him a couple of times before and when you get an invite like that it's an opportunity you jump at.

So I went down just really looking forward to spending the day there. We sat next to the Prince in the formal dinner beforehand, with all the dignitaries, and it was a great experience. But it was when I went out to watch the game and saw the boys run out that I started to think about what I had done.

My Blues team-mate and good friend Gethin Jenkins

had been made captain for the day and in the lead up to the game he'd asked me if I was sure about quitting. It was kind of an approach on behalf of the caretaker coach, Nigel Davies, to see if I might change my mind. But I had been adamant that I wasn't coming back. I didn't even think about it, because it was such a short space of time between then and the World Cup. I was happy with the decision I had made.

But now here I was at the Millennium Stadium, Wales were playing the world champions and I was sat in the stand. A lot of my mates were still in the team and I couldn't help but feel I should still be out there playing. I realised that I did miss it then, the whole atmosphere, and I went away from there with second thoughts.

I didn't have much time to dwell on things however, because a couple of days later I was heading up to London to play for the Barbarians against the Springboks. Looking back, that Baa-Baas experience was one of the best weeks of my rugby career. I had played for the famous invitation side once before, almost 10 years previously, in a pretty low game against East Midlands at Northampton, but this was a different world.

I turned up and I was surrounded by all these greats of the game, people like Justin Marshall, Jason Robinson, Jerry Collins, Matt Giteau and Joe Rokococo. I was there with my Blues team-mate Tom Shanklin and we were like little kids, just sitting there looking round us – typical Welsh boys. We're not the most confident as a breed and we were a bit overawed by it all, but it was to be an unbelievable week and I loved every minute of it.

When I had played against East Midlands all those

years ago, that was up and back in a day. But this time we were in a five-star hotel in Park Lane. I found myself sharing with Justin Harrison, the controversial Wallaby second row who had been the scourge of the Lions on the 2001 tour of Australia. I had never met him before and only really knew about him through his reputation as an abrasive, pumped-up character out on the field. So when I saw my name next to his, I thought, 'Oh my God, Justin Harrison! What a great week I've got ahead of me.' But he was an absolutely top bloke off the field. He was really good company and a real good guy and I had a great time with him.

The whole week was absolutely classic Barbarians. Let's just say there was a lot of socialising done between the Tuesday and the Thursday. In fairness to the boys, though, they were quite professional on the Friday! Usually during an international week, everything is so formal and structured, but this was real old-school. That's what I loved about it really. It was such a refreshing change.

Training consisted of doing a few line-outs, playing a little bit of touch, and the rest was down to the natural talent in the side – and there was plenty of that. Alongside me in the back row were Collins and the Aussie Rocky Elsom, and at half-back you had Marshall and Giteau, which was a dream, with Ma'a Nonu at 12 and Rockocko and Robinson out wide.

These were players I had watched and admired for years, so to actually get a chance to play with them was brilliant. Running out with them at Twickenham to take on South Africa was a fantastic experience to cap a brilliant week and the fact that we won the game just added to everything.

We really clicked as a team and things went pretty well for me personally, as I was named Man of the Match. The Baa-Baas traditionally play an open game and you've got a licence to try things you would probably never try if you were playing for your country. That kind of game probably suits me a lot. Things came off for us and it was a great experience. I look back on it as one of the big highlights of my career. It had a real international feel and it made me realise that perhaps I could still play at that level.

Coming away I was thinking, 'God, I am really going to miss this.' That's when the doubts really set in. I got back home and a lot of people started questioning my decision and saying that I had shown I could obviously still play at that level. But even then I didn't contemplate a return. I just thought that it had been a nice swan song and a good way to go out. I thought that was definitely it.

Even though I was starting to rue my decision, there was no way I was going to go with cap in hand and ask for my Wales place back. I am pretty stubborn and my attitude was that I had made my bed and I had to lie in it.

By this stage, Wales had a new coach in the New Zealander Warren Gatland, who had enjoyed huge success with Wasps. There was some speculation that he might like to have me back on board and a lot of people were asking if he had rung me, but I hadn't heard from him at all. I wasn't waiting for the phone call or anything. There was no reason to think that he would want me there and I just assumed he was looking to move on.

But then, early in the new year, my life took a dramatic turn. It was Rob Howley – the Blues backs coach who was about to do the same job with Wales – who first let something slip when he asked if Warren had rung me. I said no and asked why, but Rob just said, 'Never mind'. I thought it was just him winding me up.

But then a couple of days later, I came home to find there was a message on my answer machine. I switched it on and I heard: 'It's Warren Gatland here, can you give me a call back?' It didn't take a rocket scientist to work out what that was about. I gave him a call and he asked if I fancied meeting up for a coffee, which we did at Wales' base at the Vale of Glamorgan hotel just outside Cardiff.

As soon as I'd heard the message, I'd started thinking I really wanted to be part of it all again, because the build-up to the Six Nations championship had started and all the talk was about who was going to be in the squad. So when I met up with him, I wouldn't say my mind was made up, but I definitely went in there with a positive mind-set.

I sat down with him and from the first moment, it was typical Gats – as I was to come to know him. There was no gloss put on it, nothing fanciful. It was just a case of 'I think you can still do a job for us and I'd love you to be part of the squad.' He went on, 'I won't lie to you, it's not going to be easy. You'll work harder than you've probably ever worked before. But I'll guarantee you'll enjoy it and we'll have success.'

My first reaction was that he was a real down-to-earth genuine bloke, while his record spoke wonders. There was also talk of the Wasps head coach Shaun Edwards coming on board along with Rob Howley and I knew in my heart of hearts they were going to do well because all the ingredients were there. The players were certainly there. So to be given the chance to be part of that was hugely tempting, but I told Warren I'd have to go away to think about it.

When I'd decided to retire, I probably hadn't taken as much advice as I should have. It was more of an emotional decision based on a tough 18 months with Wales, so I really wanted to think this one through properly.

I spoke to Sam and asked what she thought and she just said I should do what I felt was best. Then I spoke to a few people whose opinions I really respect, like David 'Dai' Young, the Blues coach, who was really supportive, while the ex-players I spoke to all said it's a short career anyway and you don't want make it any shorter.

My heart definitely wanted to do it, but just to make sure I sat down and wrote down the pros and cons. My family was a big issue because I was concerned about spending a lot of time away from them. But Gats had explained we weren't going to be in camp as much as in the past, so that helped on that front. The only other con was the amount of stick I would get for coming out of retirement.

As I looked at my list, the rest were all just positives.

So my mind was made up and I told Sam. She was great about it and just said, 'I knew you were going to do that anyway!' I rang Warren to accept his offer on the Sunday night and when it came out the next morning that I was back, my phone started going non-stop with calls, messages and texts. I had to switch it off in the end.

I hadn't really told any of the Cardiff players, so when I walked back into training, I took a hell of lot of stick there. Absolutely everyone was taking the mickey out of me, but that was a small price to pay for what lay in store.

I was pretty much straight into camp with Wales, because the Six Nations was just around the corner. On our first day, there was a meeting called for 9.30 in the morning and you were thinking, 'Here we go, a two hour meeting on protocols, the same stuff you have with every new management team'. But it wasn't like that at all.

Normally when you have a new coaching set-up, you have all these power-point presentations, but this was very different. It was just a case of 'Right, this is what I expect from you'. Warren was very straight-forward and to the point and I remember Shaun was just sat there at the front glaring at everyone. He said his piece and you could see all the boys' backs straightening.

From day one, the message was if we were going to be successful we were going to have to start working harder than anyone else. As a player, it was quite refreshing and very different. With some coaches in the past, it felt like a teacher and school-kid scenario, but this felt like an adult conversation with no gloss put on it. There was straight talking and a clear message. There were no grey areas and you knew straight away where you stood.

As a player, when a new coach comes in everyone is on edge and nervous and not sure how to be. You are thinking to yourself, 'Should I relax here, should I have a laugh, should I crack a joke?' I think Gats sensed that in us. He just said, 'Look, relax, we are in this together.'

If that approach was different, then his training sessions were a real eye-opener. Just the length of them was bizarre for us. Every coach has a different philosophy on how long you should train for. The norm is that you are out there for around 75 to 90 minutes. But that's not the Gatland way.

He'd say 45 minutes and that's how long we would be there – not a minute longer. But while the sessions were a lot shorter, the intensity was really up a notch. The ball-in-play time during a match is about 45 minutes and I think he wants to make the training harder than the game, so that when you get into a game it's easier. That's the whole philosophy. It caught us by surprise at first because we'd never trained that short before and another big change was the amount of weights sessions in the gym. But it worked.

As a coaching team, the new group proved to be a great mix. Gats is very hands on for a head coach. He does a lot with the forwards and likes to coach the contact area. Robin McBryde does the line-out and the scrums, but Gats helps there as well. Rob Howley does the backs, Neil Jenkins works on the kicking and Shaun handles the defence. Previously Tuesday had been our defence day, but with Shaun we would do defence every day. Yet they were short, sharp bursts which, as a player, is brilliant. You are constantly refreshed and topped up that way.

Most of the boys are younger than me and a lot of them probably don't remember Shaun as a rugby league star with Wigan and Great Britain. But at that time, in the early '90s, I was at that age – about 15 or 16 – when I was really interested in rugby league. So for me, to have this legend in front of me was something else.

The first thing you noticed was that he was very intense. A few of the boys had it in the neck the first couple of mistakes they made, but Shaun doesn't just shout and bawl for the sake of it. What he says makes sense. He's hugely knowledgeable on the game. People sometimes think he is just shouting and screaming all the time and we are scared of him. But the truth is we have got total respect for him. If he's shouting and screaming, it's because you've made a mistake and he doesn't want you to let the side down, so he does it for a reason.

We didn't have long to prepare for the Six Nations and before we knew it we were heading up to Twickenham for our opening fixture against England.

Going up there, we didn't really know what to expect of ourselves. Warren had picked 13 Ospreys, with myself and the Scarlets winger Mark Jones the only exceptions. That raised quite a few eyebrows, but you could sense the week before that that's the way it might go because we had a new defensive policy, with the 'blitz' defence that Shaun favours, and the Ospreys boys were comfortable with it. So you had an inkling that might happen, because defence was such a huge part of our game-plan going up there. It was a brave and bold decision, but that wasn't to be the last of those during the championship.

In truth, we went up to Twickers with more hope than expectation. We hadn't won up there for 20 years and, at the end of the day, England had just got to the World Cup final, while we didn't even get out of our group, so they should have been favourites and it started off like that. We perhaps weren't quite sure of what we were trying to do and we spent most of the first half on the ropes.

Looking back on the game, the period just before half time was huge. Our hooker, Huw Bennett, just managed to get his hand in to deny their winger Paul Sackey a try and we stopped the two driving line-outs that followed that. If England had scored then, they would probably have been done and dusted. But you've got to give the guys credit. We dug in there and got to half-time.

The message from Gats then was 'Don't panic'. He said we hadn't played at all yet and that once we kept a bit of ball and did start playing we would cause them problems. He proved to be spot on because it all just clicked in the second half.

Our young fly-half James Hook did brilliantly for our first try, showing great feet and skinning a couple of defenders to put Lee Byrne in, while Mike Phillips was involved three times in our second. He made the clearing kick, he raced up field to charge down Iain Balshaw and he finished it off by scoring in the corner. It was just a great effort from him.

In the space of a few minutes, the whole momentum of the game had changed. Everything we were doing was paying off and they were making mistakes. We just grew in confidence and things started coming off. It's an amazing thing momentum.

What was really pleasing then was the way we shut the game down at the end, picking and going through the forwards, which is normally what England would do to us. That was something we had worked on for the previous fortnight in training, just looking after the ball, and it paid off.

When the final whistle went, I was just in shock that we had actually won. My very first championship game had been against England at Twickenham ten years earlier, when it was still the Five Nations. We'd lost that one 60-26 and I'd suffered quite a few dark days at HQ over the years.

So to actually win there was something very special. I'd beaten England a couple of times at home which was great, but to actually go to Twickenham and win – which no Welsh team had done since 1988 – was a huge feat for us. What made it all the sweeter was thinking that I could have been stuck in the house watching it on TV if I hadn't come out of retirement. To be part of that victory made it look a pretty good decision straight away! It really was a surreal feeling, given that just a few weeks earlier I'd been expecting to be a spectator. It flicked through my mind that it would have been so frustrating not to actually be part of it.

As you can imagine, the mood in the dressing room was really jubilant. That was the first time Shaun gave us his version of an old Drifters song, which was to become a bit of an anthem for us during the championship. I think he expected us all to have a song, but we didn't. We usually just chuck the iPod on the speakers. So when nobody responded when Shaun said, 'Give us a song', he said, 'Right then, I'll give you one' and started singing 'Saturday Night at Movies'. I'm not sure if all the lads knew the song, but I did because someone used to sing it on the bus years ago when I was with Pontypridd Youth. That made me feel pretty old all of a sudden!

It would have been easy for us to get carried away, because after all we were the first group of Welshmen to win in England for 20 years. We knew there would be loads of euphoria back home, but there was a massive message from all of us that we had a huge game the week after against Scotland. So it was a case of keeping our feet on the ground. We had a bit of a dinner and it was straight back on the bus to the Vale of Glamorgan.

We all expected the same side to be picked to face the Scots as we'd just beaten England up there. In the past, it would have been a case of 'same again' after a big win like that. But Gatland shocked everyone by making a number of changes, including replacing Mark Jones with my young Blues team-mate Jamie Roberts, and dropping the Scarlets' back row forward Alix Popham from the 22 altogether.

It surprised the boys because the two lads hadn't really played badly. I think the coaches weren't happy with Alix because he'd given a couple of penalties away, but he's still had an aggressive game after coming on as an early sub for the injured Jonathan Thomas, while Mark had had a couple of bangs on the head but didn't really do anything wrong.

So it was a huge statement by the coaches about the standards expected from everybody. I certainly didn't see it coming. It was a case of making it clear who was in charge. It would have been easy to say, 'Great boys, you've just beaten England', but in the debrief there was a lot of things pointed out as being unacceptable, especially in the first 50 minutes, and we were told in no uncertain terms that we needed to do better.

Warren provided further evidence that he was going to do things his way by swapping the Millennium Stadium changing rooms around ahead of the Scotland game. He said he didn't like the lay-out of the home one and that the away one was a much better set-up. Us old traditionalists weren't so sure. As a player, you get used to your home changing room. I had been used to changing in the same spot for a long time. But his response to our concerns was 'It hasn't been so successful for you, has it?' and you couldn't really argue with that. So it was off to a new home. It was a bit strange to go up the stairs and go left instead of right after entering the stadium, but at the end of the day it's what happens out on the pitch that really matters and that side of things was to go pretty well.

There was to be yet another indication of Warren's bold decision-making during the game against Scotland. It felt comfortable enough out there, but we just couldn't pull away from them and after an hour the game was in the balance with us ahead by just two points.

That was the cue for Gats to really shake things up again by taking off his 8, 9 and 10 – our skipper Ryan Jones and our two half-backs, Mike Phillips and James Hook – with Gareth Delve, Dwayne Peel and Stephen Jones coming on.

It was a huge decision. How many coaches would do that – take off your captain and your half-backs with 20 minutes to go? But it worked. All the guys who came on played really well and we pulled clear with Shane Williams sealing the victory by adding to his first-half try with a spectacular touchdown. When I saw the ball in his hands about 40 metres out, you could see what he was trying to do straight away. It was a phenomenal effort as he left defenders for dead, contorting his body to touch down one-handed in the corner. Perhaps his toe was in touch, perhaps it wasn't, but it deserved to be a try and it was a key moment for us in securing the win.

That victory was all the more special for me for a couple of reasons. For one thing, I had taken over the captaincy after Ryan went off. Now I hadn't had a great record as Wales skipper. In fact, I'd lost all five games in charge, which had led some of my mates to jokingly dub me 'Captain Crap'. So it was a nice feeling to be at the helm at the end of this one and finally get a win.

I was also named Man of the Match afterwards and I was particularly pleased with that as it was my first game back at the Millennium. Things went quite well that day and I was really chuffed to get the award. It was further proof that I had made the right decision in coming back.

I must admit, at half-time at Twickenham, I had been thinking, 'What have I done?' But after two games, I couldn't have dreamed for anything better. I'd beaten England in Twickenham, then been Man of the Match against the Scots and claimed a first win as skipper. I felt like pinching myself, to be honest.

Next up was Italy in Cardiff and that proved to be another comfortable victory in the end. I remember at half-time a couple of boys were quite edgy about it because it was pretty tight. But I remember Gats saying, 'Boys, we will blow them away in the last 30 minutes. Don't panic, we will be fine. Just keep doing what we are doing.' And we was right, we did blow them away.

Tom Shanklin set the ball rolling with an interception try, which was great for him on his 50th cap, Lee Byrne was excellent at full-back and Shane scored another brilliant brace of tries, so it was job done really.

Now we were one game away from the Triple Crown, with a trip to Dublin ahead of us. The build-up to that game was dominated by talk about the two opposing coaches, Gats and Eddie O'Sullivan, who had once worked together with Ireland. As players, we didn't know too much about it. We had obviously heard the rumours that they didn't get on from way back and there was a huge focus on them, which is quite good as a player because it deflects everything from the actual game. It was all centred on those two. But I didn't sense that Gats was any more intense. He is such a laid back character that it didn't seem to affect him.

It was a similar situation to Twickenham in that none of us had ever been out to Dublin and won. It was a place we hadn't had any success and we knew it was a huge game. It was also the first time any of us had played at Croke Park as well, so it was a case of going into the unknown.

Obviously there was a lot of hype about the new venue, but I wouldn't say it was intimidating. It's one of those stadiums that's so impressive it kind of inspires you as an away player. It's just an honour and a privilege to play there with all the history that goes with it.

Ireland made the better start and Shane Horgan was only an inch or so away from scoring, but Mike Phillips just managed to get underneath him. That was kind of a turning point and it shows what a fine line there is between success and failure. As it went on, we got more and more into the game and had a few opportunities to score but couldn't quite take them. Then just before half-time Mike went from hero to villain when he was sin-binned. We were up against it now, but Shane went to scrum-half and was awesome there for 10 minutes. It was a case of battening down the hatches and keeping the ball while Mike was off, which is what the pack and Shane did brilliantly.

Then, midway through the half, it was my turn to see yellow when I was carded for a trip on the Irish scrum-half, Eion Reddan. It had been my fault initially that their No 8, Jamie Heaslip, was able to break through. He should have been my man, but I was so fixed on Brian O'Driscoll, thinking he was going to get the ball, that I made the mistake in the defensive line for them to go through. Then Reddan whizzed past me on a supporting run and I knew there was no way I was going to catch him. I thought I had to do something, so instinctively I took his legs away.

It's not something I'm proud of but, to be honest, I can't believe I got caught. I was thinking I'd got away with it, but then the referee Wayne Barnes blew up. He shouldn't have seen it because it was behind the play, but in all fairness he is a top ref and he did spot it. As soon as the whistle went, I started walking off because I knew I was going. I thought sin-bin straight away. It was a horrible feeling because the game was still really in the balance. I couldn't defend myself in any way or say it was an unjustified yellow. I was bang to rights. It was a long walk to the chair and a long 10 minutes sat there.

Fortunately I got back on just in time to savour another piece of match-winning magic from Shane. I carried the ball up, then from my ruck it went to Shane and he produced a fantastic finish. Everyone knows he's got great balance, feet and speed, but he's deceptively strong as well. For that try, he went between Andrew Trimble and Tommy Bowe, who are two big strong defenders. It wasn't as though he just waltzed around a prop. You are talking two quality outside backs and he just made them look foolish, handing off Trimble on the way. We are so lucky that we've got someone that special in our side.

At the end of the game, it was a bit of a repeat of the England match in the way we kept the ball and ran down the clock, albeit for a fair bit longer this time. We killed the clock off brilliantly, with the forwards just picking and going. It wasn't the prettiest to watch, but I don't think any Welshman would complain.

To be honest, though, I can't remember too much about it. I'd had two clouts in that game – an elbow in the jaw off their prop and then a bump on the back of the head – so I can't really remember much of the last five minutes. I do know I've never been in so much pain in my life though.

After the final whistle, the boys were all celebrating on the pitch, but I just wanted to get off because I was feeling terrible. I remember feeling sick in the dressing room afterwards because I was bit concussed and when the boys went on to the dinner, I stayed in the hotel with Huw Bennett who had pulled out of the game through illness. So I wasn't at my best, but to win the Triple Crown – and in Ireland as well where I'd never won before – was still a great feeling that more than made up for a bit of a sore head.

That left just one more match – at home to France – between us and the Grand Slam, which obviously brought back memories of the Slam we'd won in Cardiff three years earlier. In 2005, our last game had been against Ireland and everyone kind of assumed we were going to win. It was seen as a foregone conclusion and that it was meant to be.

But I think a lot of people doubted us for this one. France had picked their strongest side and people thought we were going to struggle. There was a sense from the public that they didn't know if we are going to beat them and that it might be a game too far. A lot of people were saying as long as we keep it within 20 points, which is what we needed to do to win the championship. There was expectation and hope but it certainly wasn't seen as a foregone conclusion as it had been three years ago. Still everyone was massively excited and it was brilliant to go through it all again.

It was a very different kind of day, mind you. In 2005, the weather had been beautiful and thousands of people had gathered outside the civic centre in Cardiff to watch the game on a big screen. But this time it was pouring down and they had to cancel the big screen. It was a 5.30pm kick-off as well, so it was a pretty long day. The fans had been out all day and some of them were a bit worse for wear and they were looking fairly wet and bedraggled. But the support was as passionate as ever and the bus journey to the ground was just as memorable as it had been in 2005. In some ways, that was the best thing about the day. To see all those crowds and think they are there to watch you play is an unbelievable feeling, but it's also daunting in some respects.

When we got to the ground, the message from everyone within the group was just to keep doing what we had been doing. It was a case of 'Let's not change just because it's a big game. Just do what you do best and do what you've done for rest of the Six Nations and we'll be fine.' That was it really. There's not a whole lot needs to be said before a game like that. The boys are so up for it. If anything, you've got to try and bring them down a peg or two, just to make sure they are clear in their minds.

When the game got under way, it soon became clear that we were going to have our work cut out if we were to complete the Slam. We were really under the cosh in the first half and didn't have a hell of a lot of the ball. It goes without saying the French pack was huge, but their back-line was massive as well. For me as a flanker, when you are looking up and their backs are all bigger than you, you are thinking this could be a long day.

We just couldn't get the ball in that first half, so we spent most of the time defending. Our defence had been good throughout the championship, but this was when it really came into its own. I've watched the game a couple of times since and the organisation of our defence was brilliant. The boys made an incredible amount of tackles. From 1 to 15, it's probably the best defensive game a Welsh team has ever put together.

Initially, France tried to pick and go around the ruck and maul area. When they didn't get any joy from that, they started throwing it wide, but we held firm out there as well. We even kept them out when we were down to 14 men after Gavin Henson got sin binned just before half-time. That was tough against France, who are as good an attacking side as anyone on their day, but we managed it.

Going into the second-half, the game was in the balance, as had been the case with all of our matches during the championship. But once again, it was time for Shane to tip the balance. There didn't seem that much on when the ball went loose in midfield, but Shane only needs half a chance. We've all seen his ability with the ball in hand, but he's a brilliant football player as well, which he showed now. He put in a great kick and then showed his gas to get to the ball for the touchdown ahead of a couple of defenders. It was an awesome opportunist try and it was fitting that he should claim the score that took us away from them. It was also a fitting way for him to break Gareth Thomas' record and become Wales' all-time leading try scorer.

It really was a special effort, but it didn't come as any surprise to me, because Shane is probably the most talented player I've ever played with. He's just got everything and it's been a privilege to play alongside him. Everything he touched during the championship seemed to turn to gold. He was phenomenal and he continued in the same vein on the summer tour of South Africa, which I missed through injury. He's got the ability to create things out of nothing in a way that only he can.

That record-breaking try against the French must have been really sweet for him, but my own magic moment was still to come. There were just a couple of minutes left and we were on the attack in their 22 after Mark Jones had gone virtually the length of the field on an amazing run. I went to scrum-half at a ruck and then when the ball popped out, it all just opened up for me. I saw a little gap and went through it and suddenly there was this huge space in front of me with nothing between me and the line. I was thinking, This can't be happening, it's wrong. I honestly thought the ref was going to blow up. But the whistle didn't blow and I just kept going and touched down.

When I turned round and just saw all the boys sprinting towards me it was just a phenomenal feeling. There was a sense of relief and joy from all us knowing that was it, that we'd done it.

Nothing like that has ever kind of happened to me before. I'd come close in the Fiji game at the World Cup when I scored a late interception try to put us in front, but they came back to snatch the win. This was different. There was no coming back for the French and I had scored the try that sealed the Slam. To put the icing on the cake like that was an awesome feeling. It really was a dream comes true. I was named Man of the Match afterwards and it was nice to get that, but it was so difficult to pick anyone out because everyone played so well. It's the mark of a good side that the bigger the game the better you play and we all stood up that day, so it's a big pat on the back to all the boys from 1 to 22. They gave absolutely everything and for my part I was certainly feeling it at the final whistle.

I have never been so tired after a game. I was just out on my feet. I remember on the podium for the trophy presentation, when the boys were all jumping up and down, I was just standing there. I literally didn't have the energy to move. I don't know if it's my age, but I was just absolutely knackered – both emotionally and physically drained.

In the evening, there was an official function at the Hilton Hotel with the wives and girlfriends and then, the same as in 2005, we went to the pub in the Brains brewery for a private party. We had a couple of glasses of champagne in there and all the boys went out into Cardiff - apart from me! I went back on the bus with Sam, the coaching team and the trophy. I had just jumped on the bus first, thinking there would be a few boys heading back, but none of them did. They all went out for the night. So it was just me on the bus. I had a load of stick for that afterwards. I guess it's me showing my age! But while I might not have had the wildest of nights, I couldn't have been any happier. It was all the sweeter because of the realisation that I might have missed out on it all.

I suppose it was a risk coming back. Things could have gone badly wrong and it could have been a really bad decision. I could have been made to look a fool. I'm not going to name names, but I remember one person saying to me "Look be careful if you go back, you could go to Twickenham, get stuffed and be left hang out to dry".

But I was really fortunate that I came into a side that played so well and I kind of just went along with the ride. In sport, it's all about timing and a lot of it is luck. I just happened to be in the right place at the right time. I just feel so privileged and lucky to have got a second chance – and it simply couldn't have turned out any better. To go to Twickenham and win for the first time in 20 years, to go to Dublin and win the Triple Crown, to win another Grand Slam and score the clinching try – somebody must have been up there looking over me.

A lot of people have asked me how on earth we managed to turn things round so quickly and go from World Cup flops to Grand Slam winners in the space of six months. For me, there were a couple of key factors. To start with, we had two massive players back in Ryan Jones and Gavin Henson. They are hugely influential. Gav's record speaks for itself. He's never lost a Six Nations game that he's started, while Ryan had a huge influence as well as skipper. They are two British Lions standard players, so having them back was vitally important.

I also think we became mentally stronger as a group. That got instilled in us by the coaches – the confidence that we were good players and as good as these sides we were playing against. Perhaps we had kind of doubted ourselves a little bit before.

As for what the new coaches added, I would say intensity, clarity and organisation. You can use all of those words. They also brought the best out of individuals. Players like the Ospreys full-back Lee Byrne just came from nowhere and was absolutely phenomenal. The coaches got the best out of the players and got them to play to their potential by whatever means was necessary.

We'd won the 2005 Grand Slam by playing a great brand of rugby that was brilliant to watch, but this was a more professional, organised way of winning it and that was just so un-Welsh. We proved a lot of people wrong by playing that way and proved to ourselves more importantly. We weren't sure if we could play that way and defend that way, but we did – and that's down to the coaches giving us belief that we could.

It was different to 2005 in that this came from nowhere. In 2005, we'd been building up to success for a while, but we hadn't shown a glimpse of playing anything like we did in 2008. I think it's important now we realise there is still a lot of hard work to be done and that we learn the lesson from what happened after 2005 and kick on from the success this time.

Looking back, I wouldn't say one Grand Slam side was better than the other one. They are different teams. I think if they were to play against each other, it would probably be stalemate. One team was so good at attacking and the other was so good at defending. It would be a draw, but a great game to watch. And I guess I'd be pretty busy, playing on both sides!

On a personal note, it was great to win one Slam, but to win two, well there's only a few of us that can actually say that. It totally vindicated my decision to come back and hopefully there's still a bit more to come from me yet. One thing's for sure, I won't be retiring again any time soon!

## chapter 1

# the red rollercoaster

The whole of my Wales career has been something of a rollercoaster ride, with extreme highs and desperate lows coming in pretty much equal measure.

Just look at recent times. In the space of four years, we've had two Grand Slams, but in between those you had the whole Ruddockgate saga – of which more later – and the World Cup disaster of 2007.

That latter failure was all the more painful for me, because at the time I thought it was the end of my international career, as I had decided to retire from the Test arena after the World Cup.

In my dreams, my last game for Wales was going to be at the Stade de France in Paris as part of a World Cup-winning team. Instead it was in Nantes, against Fiji, and it was to end with us bombing out of the tournament and Gareth Jenkins losing his job as coach.

Having made up my mind to quit, I had been desperate to finish my 11-year test career on a high. But unfortunately, the tournament was to finish on a real low for us. So where did it all go wrong? To my mind, it all goes back to the fall-out from the 2005 Grand Slam. That championship clean-sweep – Wales' first since 1978 – stands out as a real highlight of my career and the memories will stay with me forever.

But it was to have another legacy, one which ultimately culminated in that dark day at the Stade de la Beaujoire in Nantes in October 2007.

We won the Grand Slam playing a particular brand of fluid, running rugby – a style that I truly believe suits us best as a nation – the 'Welsh way' as it's been dubbed. However, the following season, we found ourselves missing a lot of key players through injury and we didn't do too well. Suddenly, everyone was saying the way we were trying to play couldn't work any longer. The argument went that our opponents had worked us out so we had to change the way we were playing.

Now, I'm the first to admit that the game moves on and you've got to develop as a team, but at the time I honestly didn't think we had to change that much. Yet it was to be a case of all change.

By the end of the 2006 Six Nations, the last of the southern hemisphere architects of the 'Welsh way' had gone, with skills specialist Scott Johnson and former head coach Steve Hansen and fitness guru Andrew Hore returning Down Under. In came a new home-grown management team, headed up by long-serving Llanelli coach Gareth Jenkins, who had finally landed the job he had wanted for so long.

Before I go any further, I want to say that I've got a lot

of respect for Gareth and that I think he's a genuinely great guy. But I just feel that perhaps he tried to change too much too soon, when there wasn't really a need to do it.

When a new coach comes in, they are obviously going to have their own ideas and their own views on taking the team forward. That's fine. But I just think there was a knee-jerk reaction because we hadn't had a successful Six Nations in 2006. It was difficult for us as a group of players, because for three or four years we had worked so hard on developing a particular style and then we found ourselves having to move away from it. It was as if three quarters of the way through a journey, we were told to head to a different destination.

From midway through 2002, we had worked on avoiding contact and playing to our natural strengths by keeping the ball alive and moving it wide, with as much of an emphasis on the forwards' handling as on the backs. But Gareth wanted us to be a more physical side, with the onus on the forwards to act as carriers.

Looking back, we spent a hell of a lot of time in training doing contact work, really climbing into each other and smashing each other. It was more than we'd ever done before under any coach during my time involved with Wales.

The older you get as a player, the less you like doing that in training – you just want to play. I think there is a time and a place for getting physical and if you get something out of it, then fine. But, sometimes, I thought we were doing it for the sake of it. We were also doing it instead of other skill-based work that would have benefited us more.

The physical, direct approach had been successful for Gareth at Llanelli, where he had based a lot of his strategy around big men like Scott Quinnell, Martyn Madden and Salesi Finau smashing the ball up. But at international level, it's different. In those matches, you are coming up against players who are just as big and powerful as you and often bigger and more powerful. We are not the biggest nation in the world physically and I don't think it suits us to get dragged into a confrontational, set-piece game.

But when Gareth came in, I felt there was an attempt to try and copy the power game of the likes of England, South Africa and France. I just don't think that's a natural game for the Welsh and, for the majority of players in the squad, it was an alien way to play.

In Wales, we have a tendency to look at other sides, see where they've been successful and think we must copy them to get results. But just because one side has been successful, it doesn't mean that replicating their technique will do you any good.

I feel you've got to play to your strengths and our strength is that we've got a lot of people who are natural rugby players with great skills – people like Shane Williams, who showed in the 2008 Slam what he could do when given the freedom to express himself. So let's try and build on what we are good at rather than trying to become something we are not and never will be.

The more physical approach wasn't the only big change under Gareth. In the late summer of 2006, he and his assistant Nigel Davies went to South Africa to watch the Tri-Nations tournament and they realised that those teams, especially New Zealand, were kicking a hell of a lot. So again, it was time for us to become copycats. It did make sense to try and develop our kicking, as it's very useful to have a big kicking game in your armoury.

But we were suddenly being asked to kick an awful lot when it was something we weren't used to doing that much, so it was always going to be difficult to bring it in over a short space of time.

It's like anything in rugby. You perform at your best when you don't think about it and just play by instinct.

The boys were being told to kick here, there and everywhere and it just wasn't natural for them. The first thought from the likes of Gareth 'Alfie' Thomas and Kevin Morgan would be to keep the ball in hand and run. It always has been. To suddenly change that mentality takes time, and unfortunately, with the next international challenge on the horizon, time was one thing we didn't have.

I don't want to give the impression that the 2005 Grand Slam was based purely on running from everywhere and throwing the ball around for 80 minutes. Yes, we did play some great rugby and we did score some great tries. But we did the dirty stuff as well, the nitty-gritty work up front and we also had the kicking covered by Stephen Jones and Gavin Henson.

The key was that everyone understood what needed to be done in any given situation. Under Gareth and Nigel, things just became a bit confused.

In meetings, they would emphasise that they wanted us to get the ball in hand and play with width, because we have got dangerous runners and attackers. But then when we went out onto the paddock, we weren't really training like that. We'd just do a hell of a lot of contact, piling into each other. This is where our confusion came from.

You'd go into games with an idea that you wanted to play a certain way, but because you'd been training so much the other way, you'd be caught between two stools. We were talking about playing the Welsh way, but training to play a tighter driving game and a kicking game. There was a sense of confusion about how we were supposed to play. In the end, we played like we trained, with lots of endeavour and commitment, but that contact game just didn't really work for us.

A number of the senior players, myself included, did try and express our views about this. There were a few times where I said I felt we were doing far too much meaningless contact, while other players made other points. We were concerned about a few off-the-field matters as well, but the management group took us as being negative rather than constructive. It felt as though they only wanted to hear positive comments. In the end, I felt I might as well give up trying to express my views, because it just wasn't worth it, and I know other players felt the same.

One thing a lot of people outside the camp probably didn't realise was that it was Nigel who did most of the coaching. Gareth largely did the overseeing and would give the emotional spiel. All the tactical stuff would be done by Nigel.

He ran the show in terms of the coaching and he would be the one doing the majority of the talking at meetings. Most of the public wouldn't have been aware of that.

The only time Gareth really did any hands-on coaching was before the World Cup warm-up match against England in August 2007 when our forwards coach Robyn McBryde was up at the National Eisteddfod in Mold. Normally, Nigel would do the backs and our attack, Robin would do all the set-piece work with the forwards, Rowland Phillips would do the defence and Neil Jenkins worked with the kickers.

You feel for the head coach sometimes at international level, because they take all the flak when things go wrong, but it's very much a collective effort with the team management and the players all having a part to play.

Gareth's time in charge began with a summer tour of Argentina in 2006, which I didn't go on, and then came the autumn internationals, where we came from behind to earn a creditable draw with Australia. That result offered some hope for the 2007 Six Nations, but, for the most part, it was to be a hugely frustrating campaign.

It began with a defeat at home to Ireland, when the little things just didn't go our way and the bounce of the ball went against us. People talk about the luck of the Irish and that was never more evident than on that Sunday afternoon at the Millennium Stadium.

But while there were some plusses to come out of that game, the same couldn't be said about our next match, against the Scots up in Edinburgh. That proved the low point of the campaign in more ways than one. It was our worst performance of the championship by some distance and we were rightly criticised for that, but what earned us the fiercest flak is what we did after the match.

Our 'crime' was to go out for a drink in a city-centre

nightclub, something that was to become headline news back home in Wales a couple of days later.

The background to the incident is that the boys hadn't had the chance to relax and let off steam for a couple of months. We'd had all the Welsh derbies over Christmas, then in January we had the Heineken Cup games and after that you are pretty much straight into the international period. It was agreed that the night of the Scotland game would be a good time to let our hair down and just relax a bit, because we didn't have a fixture the following weekend. But no one had envisaged what that Murrayfield match was going to be like.

The fact that we were out at all after such a poor performance didn't go down well in the slightest with some fans and the story ended up making the papers.

I can see why people got upset and especially given the hard time a lot of fans had been through getting up to Edinburgh, with the bad weather that weekend causing some horrendous delays. But I am a big, big believer that socialising off the field brings you together as a group of players more than anything else. I'm not saying you should do it all the time by any means, but once in a while it's just good to spend time together away from the training field.

Of course, if we'd beaten Scotland there wouldn't have been any problem at all. Nobody mentions the times when the boys went out after the French or Irish games during the Grand Slam campaign in 2005 and those were much wilder nights. But because we played so poorly, people were looking for anything to have a go at us over.

If we'd had a game six days later then fair enough, it

probably wouldn't have been the right thing to do, but our next match wasn't for another two weeks. We still had to get up for a pool recovery the next morning as well. It's not as though we were just lying there in bed all day Sunday.

When you are a professional sportsman and in the limelight you've got to accept that people are going to scrutinise your actions. But it wasn't as if we smashed the place up or were involved in a mass brawl, like the one I experienced as a young player with Pontypridd out in the French city of Brive. We were just out with the Scottish players and having some time to ourselves. It was Dwayne Peel's fiftieth cap and Simon Taylor's fiftieth for Scotland as well and we just wanted to relax and have a couple of drinks. Believe me, it was tame compared to some of the things I've seen during my career. But one or two fans didn't take kindly to seeing us out. A few comments were made and a couple of the boys made remarks back, which led to one or two people complaining to the Welsh Rugby Union and apologies being made.

Ninety-nine percent of the time, the boys will just walk away. But we are only human, and there's only so much you can take. Sometimes you will bite back and say something. It's hard to bite your tongue all the time. There's going to be instances where the boys are going to react to things that are said. It's natural. The problem is once you do it a big deal is made out of it.

As players, we hugely appreciate the efforts Welsh fans make to come and cheer us on and we realise how frustrating it must be for them when they don't get the result they are hoping for. But I don't think people always realise just how frustrated the players are as well when that happens and just how much we want to win when we play for our country. However much the supporters are hurting, we are hurting just as much when we lose. You are as frustrated as anyone and you take it more personally than anyone. It's just a horrible experience.

The journey back home as a Welsh player when you've lost out in Dublin or Edinburgh is something you wouldn't wish on your worst enemy. You go through the airport, with all the fans there, which is an absolute nightmare, because you feel guilty that you've let people down after they've had such high expectations.

Then, when you get back home, you don't want to go out anywhere. You just want to stay in. Your missus is saying, 'Come on, let's go out', but you just don't want to leave your front door. That's what it's like being a Wales rugby player after a defeat. You don't want to go to the supermarket, you don't want to see anyone, because you just end up having to explain yourself a thousand times over, trying to explain what went wrong. It's a tough time.

When you've got a game the next week and you're straight back to training, that's fine, but when you've got a couple of days off, you mull over it all and that's the worst bit. You don't sleep properly for days afterwards. It just goes round and round in your head.

That's what it was like during the majority of the 2007 Six Nations, with further defeats following out in France and Italy, leaving us staring at a whitewash, with only the England game in Cardiff left as a final shot at redemption.

Going into that final fixture, I had made my mind up that it was going to be my last Six Nations match, so I really wanted my daughter Mia to be there as she wouldn't have another chance to see her dad play in the tournament – or so I thought at the time. The day went like a dream, as we ended what had been a torrid campaign with a 27-18 victory over the old enemy and it meant so much to me that Mia was there to see it. It was also a result that gave us fresh hope for the World Cup that was coming up later in the year.

One of the big decisions facing Gareth and his back-up team in the build-up to that tournament was how to treat the summer tour to Australia and the three warm-up games against England, Argentina and France.

In the end, it was decided that a group of about 18 of us would miss the trip Down Under and stay at home to do a 12-week block of fitness work. I can totally see why it was done, because they wanted to get us in peak condition for the World Cup. But I remembered the summer of 2003 when we all went away on tour to Australia and New Zealand. We ended up getting hammered by the All Blacks, but what that trip did was to knit us together. We became really close as a squad and saw the benefits at the World Cup later that year.

It's a really difficult balancing act and hindsight is a great thing, but I think it would have been better for us if we'd all gone to Australia. You can do as much conditioning as you like and all the training in the world, but you can't replicate the game situation or being exposed to pressure moments in big matches.

When we were about four or five weeks into our training programme, we were joined by the boys who had gone on tour to Australia and it was an awkward scenario to be in. It wasn't a case of us and them, but it was just horrible because you knew some people were going to miss out on the final 30-man squad for the World Cup.

At the end of July, all 40 of us who were in the frame went out to Brittany in France for a week's training camp and, to put it mildly, training was a little bit intense. It got out of control a few times and there were a few dust-ups because of the pressure, with everyone wanting to make that final cut.

To finish off the week, we had a trial match at our training ground in Saint-Nazaire, where we were split into two teams. To a lot of the boys, it was a bit of a farce. There were about 4,000 French people there to watch, but it was right at the end of a really demanding week and boys were just chucked in to make up the numbers. The team I was in had a back row made up of me at No 8 and Adam Jones and Richard Hibbard – a prop and a hooker – on the flanks!

I'm totally against trial matches. Everyone knows each other so well and they are just trying to get one up on each other. And how can you pick somebody on just one game? But, saying that, if anybody played themselves out of the final 30 that day it was Gavin Henson. I think the coaches really wanted to take Gav to the World Cup, but the way he was in that trial there was no way you could pick him.

It was gutting for me because on his day he's a huge asset – as he's proved during two Grand Slams. He's a great player and I would go as far as to say that when he's fit and on form, Wales are a different side with him in there. He's great with the ball in hand, he can kick

60-70 metres down the field and can be as good a tackler as anyone.

When you train with someone every day, you know the ability they've got and how good they can be. There's nothing worse than seeing someone with all the talent in the world not fulfilling their potential. It's hugely frustrating. We were all thinking it would be great to have Gavin back in the squad. But you can't blame them for not taking him after that trial. So when it was announced the following week that he was being cut from the training squad, there was no surprise among the boys. You could see it coming from the time we'd had out in France. The boys knew there was no way Gavin could form part of the team.

What's been great to see is the way he's bounced back from missing out on a second World Cup – having also been left out of the squad in 2003 – to play his part in a second Grand Slam. Hopefully there will be plenty more highs to come from Gavin, because there's no questioning his ability.

If his omission from the World Cup party wasn't a surprise, then the team to play the opening warm-up game against England at Twickenham at the beginning of August certainly was.

Gareth decided to stick mainly with the boys that had been on tour Down Under and picked what was dubbed a 'second string' side.

I really was shocked at the selection. I'd expected a lot more players who were going to figure in the World Cup to be involved. If you didn't play in that game, it meant you were only going to have one-and-a-half matches before the tournament kicked off. It was kind of a missed opportunity to get some game time because there were quite a few boys who played in that England match who didn't go to the World Cup.

But I think the game was kind of an inconvenience to Gareth. He chose a second, or even a third-string side, with his attention focused on his key players sitting out the match and working on their fitness ahead of the World Cup. He thought we would get more benefit by having a couple of weeks more conditioning rather than playing.

I don't think he'd anticipated the kind of beating we ended up taking at Twickenham. If we'd put in a good performance and just lost narrowly it wouldn't have been too bad, but to go up there and get thumped 62-5 was something else. The Welsh public never likes losing to England at the best of times, but the manner of the defeat magnified everything. That scoreline was hard to bear and Gareth took a lot of flak for his team selection.

I really felt sorry for the boys who played that day. Chucked together, they only had a week to prepare before they were taken up to Twickers, so you felt for them. They were kind of lambs to the slaughter.

Our World Cup preparations couldn't have got off to a worse start really and camp wasn't a great place to be on the Monday morning. You really didn't know what to say to the boys who had played. Everyone was shocked. No one could see it coming and I think Gareth was surprised by what had happened. He took a lot of stick in the media and the defeat put a lot of pressure on everyone. Thankfully, we just managed to hold on for a win against Argentina before losing to France. With the warm-up over, it was time for the trip across the Channel and the real thing.

The build-up to our opening World Cup group match against Canada in Nantes was to be pretty eventful. By that stage, Gareth had stopped talking to the Western Mail, the national newspaper of Wales, because he was unhappy with their coverage.

The dispute came to a head at the official reception for the squad at the town hall in Saint Nazaire. It was quite a formal affair, with all the civic dignitaries present, with Gareth sitting at the front of the hall accompanied by the rest of the management team while all the official greetings were made.

Then came the questions from the press and as soon as he was asked one by a Western Mail reporter, Gareth turned his head away and refused to comment. The trouble was our French hosts didn't know the background to the situation and didn't understand what was going on. So there was this awkward silence, while the interpreter, who had been waiting to translate the reply, stood there looking bemused.

Everyone handles the press in different ways and Gareth had his own strategy, so that's fair enough. It can be hard when things get personal, which is how he saw it. He wanted to make a point and that was his way of doing it, but I'd never seen a coach do that before, so it was a bit of a surprise.

What was even more surprising, though, was what he had in store for us with his team selection to face the Canadians.

Over the summer, the big talking point had been who

would be chosen as skipper for the World Cup. Would it be our fly-half Stephen Jones, who'd been in charge the previous season, or would it be 'Alfie' – the 2005 Grand Slam and British Lions captain. Personally, I think the captaincy had been allowed to become too much of an issue. It had become a huge talking point in the press, when speculation could have been nipped in the bud a lot earlier to avoid distractions from the task at hand.

In the end, it wasn't until the day of the squad announcement, in mid-August, that Gareth made his announcement, with Alfie being handed the reins. Stephen was probably disappointed that he wasn't going to be captain because it's a huge honour. But he'd picked up an injury in that trial match out in Brittany and I think his priority was to be fit and to get to the World Cup. He is just about the nicest bloke in the world – he and Alfie get on really well, so there was no problem.

It had all been resolved, we had got out to France and everyone knew where they stood. Or so we thought. Just when it seemed as though the whole issue had been put to be bed, Gareth dropped a bombshell by announcing that our scrum-half Dwayne Peel was going to be captain against Canada, with Alfie on the bench!

We didn't see that one coming at all. It came totally out of the blue and everyone was really stunned. I think Dwayne definitely has what it takes to be Wales' captain one day, because he's got all the attributes you would want from a skipper. It was just a big shock at the time, because we all thought Alfie would be playing. I know Alfie well and he was gutted. He was like everybody else, surprised and shocked by the news.

16

I told him he was probably in the best place on the bench because the first hour was going to be a dogfight. He could then come on and make a big impact. As it happened, I was spot on, because that's exactly how it panned out.

It was our first match of the World Cup, so there were a lot of nerves which showed in our play. It was a huge game for the Canadians. They obviously targeted that we could be beaten and they really came out firing. Not long after half-time, we were losing 17-9 and on course for the worst possible start to our campaign. But that was the cue for Alfie and Stephen to come on and save the day.

There had been a lot of talk before the tournament about who should start at fly-half and it was young James Hook who had got the nod. James had been picked out as one of the players to watch in just about all the supplements and tournament guides, so there was a lot of expectation riding on him. Unfortunately, we didn't really give him a platform to express himself in that first 50 minutes against Canada, so it was always going to be difficult for him and it didn't help when his pass was intercepted for their first try.

When he was taken off, along with Kevin Morgan, we were in big trouble. But then Stephen and Alfie came on and started pulling the strings. We started to get on top and to show what we can do.

But then just as the game began to open up, I was taken off! I was hugely frustrated because we had done all the hard work and you just knew we were going to put them to bed. There was 20 minutes left, we were two scores in front, the game was going to open up and that's what I'm best at. But I got pulled off and Colin Charvis came on and did awesomely. I've never been so frustrated. The red head and the spoilt kid came out in me and I kind of threw my toys out of the pram when I came off.

That night I had really mixed emotions about the game. I was delighted that we'd won our opening fixture but very concerned about my place in the team for the next match. I was thinking they would go with the boys who had finished off the game.

It had been obvious from the way I'd reacted when I was taken off and from my manner when I got back in the changing room that I wasn't happy. So, the next day, Gareth asked me what my problem was and I told him. He insisted it was just a case of bringing on fresh legs, that there was nothing more to his decision and that I'd play the next week against Australia. I obviously felt a lot better after our conversation so I was able to turn my attentions to the Wallabies.

That match was to be played at the Millennium Stadium and it was strange coming back into the country. It was nice to get home and see the family, but it didn't really feel like the World Cup. It felt more like the autumn internationals.

On paper, the prospects looked pretty good for us. We had home advantage and the Aussies were missing their influential fly-half Stephen Larkham, who was out injured. But by half-time, we were 25-3 down and the game was over as a contest.

After that we had nothing to lose and it was a case of let's just go out and play. The new game-plan went out of the window and we reverted to our natural game. The shackles were off and we started to cause them problems. But it was just too much of a mountain to climb, and we were beaten 32-20.

There were a lot of changes made for our next game against Japan and originally I was due to be on the bench. At the eleventh hour I was drafted into the starting line-up when Jonathan Thomas was ruled out with a damaged thumb. I was more relaxed going into that game than I normally am because I hadn't had a lot of time to think. It turned out to be a good night for me as I scored two tries in a 72-18 win.

Then it was back out to France for the group decider against Fiji. I must admit that by this stage I was getting a bit sick of our base in Pornichet on the Brittany coast, about an hour's drive from Nantes.

It was our third stay there, after the training camp in July and the week or so leading up to the Canada match. The hotel was fine and the area was nice enough, but there wasn't much to do and it did become a bit boring. I generally feel it's better to stay in a city if you can because you can go for a walk and wander around the shops or just for a coffee to break up the day a bit.

But that's no excuse for what happened against Fiji.

It's since been hailed as one of the all-time great World Cup games and I guess it must have made good viewing for the neutral – but it's a match to remember for all the wrong reasons if you're Welsh.

We knew Fiji were dangerous from broken play, so the game-plan was to take them on at set-piece, spoil their ball in the line-out and attack their scrum. Yet we ended up getting dragged into a game of Sevens, which is the last thing we needed to happen. There's no one better at that in the world than the Fijians and they cut us to ribbons in the first half.

Then suddenly we started to play. We kept the ball, went through the phases and showed what we could do. We'd turned the game round, got our noses in front and it looked like we'd come through the storm, only for the Fijians to come again and go back in front.

Then, with time running out, came the moment when I thought I'd saved our bacon. As soon as their fly-half Nicky Little threw out the pass, I knew the interception was on and I went for it. Suddenly I had the ball in my hands and there was no-one between me and the line. I was something like 60 metres out, so I was thinking to myself, 'I've got some of the quickest players in the world around me – just pin your ears back and go!'

I'd like to think that throughout my career I've not had tunnel vision and that I'm quite aware of what's going on around me. But for that moment I didn't.

If you are someone like Shane Williams or Mark Jones, who've got natural gas, then you don't think anything of running in interceptions from 60 metres. But when you are somebody that's not used to it, it's a different story. I just panicked and thought I've got to get to the line as quick as I can. I was expecting a Fijian winger to cut me down at any second. It could have been a second row as they are so quick!

As I was crossing the 22, I could just see their wing Sereli Bobo out of the corner of my eye and that made me panic me even more. So when I got to the line, I just touched the ball down straight away when I should really have gone under the posts. I've had a fair bit of stick off my mates over that and I know it was something of a talking point after the game. But, at the time, I was just caught up in the moment and I didn't think anything of it. I didn't feel I was too far out, but unfortunately Stephen hit the post with the conversion.

We were still four points in front though, with only a couple of minutes left. Surely we could hold out? But the Fijians claimed the kick-off and came roaring back at us. And once again I was to find myself at the centre of the action. I tackled Viliami Delasau just short of the line and there was the ball lying between the two of us. I remember thinking to myself, 'Should I roll away or stay in here and give away the penalty.' In the end, I rolled away and they scored the try that won the game. To this day, I regret not killing that ball. It's such a fine line at moments like that.

If I'd given the penalty away, got sin-binned and they scored from the driving line-out, then I would have been the villain of the piece. But it's still in the back of my mind that I shouldn't have let that ball come out.

There was no way back from that try and a minute or so later the final whistle sounded. I just remember feeling shocked and totally gutted. We were as devastated as the Fijians were delighted. As far as I was concerned, it was the end of the road for me with Wales, so I made a point of going round all the boys to shake hands with them. It was a sad way to finish because I'd been through so much with a lot of those guys.

In a way, that last game summed up my time playing for Wales. One minute we'd been awful, the next we'd been brilliant. It was a really strange feeling in the dressing room afterwards. Everyone was just walking round in absolute shock. We hadn't expected to go out and the thought that we would be going home the next day was horrible.

For me, it was quite emotional because I thought I was never going to put the jersey on again and it wasn't the ideal way to finish, on a down, rather than with a bit of glory. We knew it was going to be a tough couple of days after that, but we didn't realise how fast things would happen.

The next morning, the top two men in the WRU, Roger Lewis and David Pickering, turned up at the team hotel, so I started to put two and two together. If they had travelled all the way out from Nantes, we had an idea of what was coming – and so it proved. Roger stood up in front of us and explained they felt it was time for Gareth to go. Then Gareth spoke to us himself. He was really dignified. He said he'd dreamed of doing the job and that he had no regrets. It was just that things hadn't worked out as he'd wanted.

It was a really sad moment and I felt really sorry for him. We were all devastated for bombing out of the tournament. This announcement meant more misery was being heaped upon us.

Let's be realistic, we knew this was the end for Gareth after getting knocked out at the group stages. I would have been amazed if he had stayed on after that. But I thought it would be done during the week of our return.

Personally, I felt he should have been allowed to come back as the coach. We went out as a squad and we should have come back as a squad. Instead, when we got back to our base at the Vale of Glamorgan hotel, on the outskirts Cardiff, Gareth got off the bus before the rest of us and just walked away on his own. It was a horrible way for it to finish. The focus was taken off the team and was put solely on Gareth, as though he carried the can for everything.

For all the mistakes I think were made along the way, I've still got a lot of respect for the guy.

I hadn't worked under him until he became Wales coach, apart from a couple of midweek games on the 2005 Lions tour to New Zealand, and I didn't know him that well.

In fact, I didn't really get to know Gareth properly until myself, him and Shane Williams went up to a Labour Party dinner at the new Wembley Stadium in July 2007. We'd been invited by Alastair Campbell, who'd been a media advisor on the Lions tour which we'd all been on together.

Gareth drove us up to London and it was the first time I got to know him outside of rugby. The event was to celebrate 10 years of sport under Labour and it was just an unbelievable do. We were in the VIP room with Tony Blair and Gordon Brown, and Shane and me were saying, 'What are we doing here?' It was totally out of our league! Mick Hucknall from Simply Red was singing live at the event and I ended up sitting next to his manager at the dinner, so he brought Mick over and he said 'nice colour hair'.

It was just an amazing function. At one point, Gareth, Shane and me went up on stage along with Sir Alex Ferguson for an auction, in which the audience bid for a day with the Welsh team and a day with Manchester

United. Someone paid £20,000 to spend the day with us, and I think the United day went for £80,000.

I spent a lot of time with Gareth over that weekend talking about things other than rugby and I came away thinking a hell of a lot of the guy. He's a great character and such an upbeat bloke.

We knew there were times when he was under a lot of pressure as coach because things weren't going that well. But you'd never think it from looking at him and it would never knock on to the players. That's a huge strength of his. He was so positive and so upbeat that sometimes he could lift you as a team and you would always have a great talk off him before you left the hotel to go to a game.

Looking back, I think it's unfair the way so much has been blamed on him. We failed as a group, yet he's the one who will always be associated with that failure. You can't put it all down to one guy. I think as players we've got to take an equal share of the responsibility. It's the million dollar question why it all went wrong.

It's been suggested that the players weren't playing for Gareth towards the end, but there was never an issue with 'player power' as far as I'm concerned. Everyone was trying to buy into everything that was being taught to us, but we couldn't implement it as well as what they wanted because we weren't used to playing in that way.

We were a group of players who had been going in one direction for quite a while and then all of a sudden we had to go another way and it was difficult. Everyone – players and management alike – gave it their best shot but it just didn't work out. At the end of the day it was a collective failure, just in the same way as one person didn't win the

Grand Slam in 2005 or 2008. It's down to everyone in the set-up.

As I say, I've been through some real highs and some real lows with Wales, but in a way that's what's made it all the more special as when you've been down the bottom, you appreciate it all the more at the top. From the day when I won my first cap as a 20-year-old against the Barbarians in August 1996, it's been a privilege and an honour to pull on that red jersey.

The best part about playing for your country is when you run out of the tunnel. The actual game is one thing, but that feeling you get when you run out onto the pitch and when you stand there for the anthem is just something else altogether. I realise more and more now just how lucky I have been to do that, because it's so many people's dream and one I have lived.

Playing for Wales is what I wanted to do from about the age of nine. If someone had said to me then that I would get just one cap I would have been more than happy.

As it turns out, I've been lucky enough to get more than 80 – and I wouldn't have missed it for the world.

# losing the ones you love

Martyn Elwyn Williams – or 'Nugget' as I've been known throughout my career – entered the world at East Glamorgan Hospital in Church Village on 1 September 1975.

For the first seven years of my life, I lived in the Rhondda valley, first in Maerdy, then Porth, then Penygraig, before finally moving down to Pontypridd. It's fair to say my family life was pretty nomadic. It was also pretty unusual.

My mother, Julie, had me when she was just seventeen and, to this day, I've never met my biological father. Like a lot of women who have a child at a young age, she ended up becoming a single parent, although she had plenty of family support around her.

Up until I was five, I lived with my mum, her three sisters – Karen, Bev and Debra – and their mother and father. It was just a terraced house and, looking back, I don't know how the hell we used to manage. My grandmother, Val, still lives in the house in Porth and, when I go back there, it's amazing to think how we all fitted in, but they were great times. Being brought up by four sisters, I was spoilt rotten to be honest and I never wanted for anything

In those early days, my father figure was my grandfather, Elwyn, which is where my middle name comes from. He was only thirty-eight when I was born. I used to call him my 'daddo' and he was what I took to be my father. When you are only four or five, you don't really understand things properly and it was just normal life as far as I was concerned. Until he died, when I was fifteen, he was the be-all and end-all for me. I used to love spending as much time as I could with him. When I started playing mini-rugby he'd always come and watch and he was a huge part of my life. He was only fifty-three when he passed away and it was very hard for me to come to terms with that loss.

When I was five, my mother married Paul, who became my step-dad. You are perhaps a little bit standoffish at first when a new person enters your life, but there was never any real conflict between Paul and I. It was fine and, from that point on, he was my father. There was no big deal about it.

Having kids of my own now, I realise how hard it must have been for him to marry someone who already had a child and I owe him a lot for the support he gave me. He sacrificed a hell of a lot so i could further my rugby career. We still see each other regularly and are usually in touch most weeks. He comes to the big games to watch me play and he sees the kids a fair bit. I'd say my relationship with him today is as strong as ever.

In February 1982, a couple of years after Paul and my mum got married, my brother Craig was born, and not long after that we moved to Paul's hometown, Pontypridd; it was a move that really opened the door to my rugby career.

Up in the Rhondda, it had all been football, but that changed when I switched to Coed-y-Lan Junior School in Ponty. I'll never forget Mr Howells, the head teacher, saying if anybody was interested in playing rugby to put their hands up. Without really thinking, I stuck mine up. I don't know why. I guess it was just because it was sport. Even if it had been cricket I would have said yes.

I got completely hooked on the game from the moment I started playing it. The coach at school was a guy called Jack Bayliss and he was running the Pontyclun mini-rugby side at the time as well. It was when I joined them that I really began to make progress. I was a stroppy little bugger when I started off – and I still can be at times today – but Jack was brilliant with me. When I was with Pontyclun, we used to go on great trips to places like London Welsh and Marlow for mini-rugby tournaments and my family always used to come and watch me play.

I was also playing for the school and, when I was nine, I was part of the Coed-y-Lan team that won the Ponty Schools Under-11 Cup. We played the final at Sardis Road, the home of Pontypridd Rugby Club, which was a huge thing for me at the time. It was a place that was to become very familiar to me over the coming years.

Another early highlight was when I was picked to play for East Wales Under-11s against West Wales at Cardiff Arms Park. From that moment on, it was my dream to play for Wales. I wasn't too bad at football either, and I used to play a fair bit of that. I even played at centre-half for the Welsh YMCA team at one point, but rugby was always the main love.

I had started out as a second row, because I was quite tall for my age, but then I was moved to No. 8. It was a man by the name of Brian Lease who was to switch me to the open-side flanker berth that was to become my home on the rugby field. Brian became my coach when I joined the Pontypridd Schools Under-15s side and he was a big influence on me for the next few years, as he was for the likes of Kevin Morgan, Gareth Wyatt and Lee Jarvis, who all went on to play for Wales. He was very much from a fitness and athletics background and he was very strict. I can still remember what he said to me when I got my letter telling me I'd been selected for Wales Under-15s. He said: 'You think you've made it don't you? Well, the hard work starts now.' That's something that's always stuck with me – you can never afford to rest on your laurels.

Brian had played on the open-side for Cardiff and he could see a No. 7 in me. I wasn't as big then for my age as I had been with the Under-11s, but I was quick and really fit. So he moved me across to the open-side and that's when I really started taking the game seriously.

Representative honours started coming my way, with caps for Wales at Under-15, Under-16 and two years early for the Under-19 team, as well as for Wales Schools, who I went on tour to Australia with in the summer of 1994 when I was eighteen. That was a fantastic trip. We had a really talented side, with future full internationals like

Leigh Davies, Nathan Thomas, Chris Anthony, Jamie Ringer, Nick Walne and John Funnell on board, and we ended up winning six of our seven matches, including the Test match against Australia in Brisbane.

By then I was already part of the set-up at Pontypridd Rugby Club, which was to be my home until 1999. I'd been playing for their youth team since I was sixteen and I'd even had a taste of first-team action on a trip to Waterloo in October 1993, a memorable experience which I detail in the next chapter.

After coming back from Australia, I made my first senior start for Ponty against South Wales Police at Sardis in September 1994 and caps followed for Wales with the Under-21s, who I had the honour of captaining a couple of times. Then, in August 1996, I fulfilled the ambition I'd had since I was nine years old when I won my first full cap against the Barbarians.

For the next few years, my career moved along pretty smoothly, first with Ponty and then Cardiff, and the caps kept coming with Wales. Life was pretty good. But then, in the autumn of 2000, life kicked me in the teeth.

Even though I was seven years older than Craig, we had always been really close. As well as being brothers, we were also the best of friends and had a great understanding. He used to love knocking about with my mates and especially when the rugby kicked in – he liked all that. He played a bit himself when he was a teenager and he was pretty good. He used to play in the centre and he was quick and a lot more powerful than I was. He played for Ynysybwl Youth and one of his big mates in the team was Rhys Thomas, who is now the hooker for Cardiff Blues and Wales. Rhys used to come around the house a fair bit and ... let's just say he's slimmed down quite a lot since those days!

While Craig was a pretty decent player, it's probably fair to say he was never the most dedicated. He was more of a social player and he enjoyed the crack with the boys. That was him all over. He just enjoyed life so much, which makes what happened to him all the more cruel.

I can still remember the day in September 2000 when I had a phone call from my mother to say that Craig had been taken into hospital because he was suffering from headaches. At that point you're obviously worried, but you're not really thinking the worst. After all, he was only eighteen. But when I went up to see him at the Royal Glamorgan Hospital that day, I knew something was badly wrong. He was trying to eat some ice cream and he couldn't get the spoon into his mouth.

They did the scan that day and when the results came back it was the worst possible news. It was cancer and it was so advanced there was nothing they could do. It was devastating news and you just couldn't believe it. He was so young.

It turned out to be melonoma, which is skin cancer, and the tumour had spread all around his brain. They said it was quite a rare condition and what really baffled them was that they could never find the source of it.

He had radiotherapy and for the first four to five weeks he wasn't too bad, but then after that he really declined and it developed a lot more quickly than had been expected. He never really asked anyone how long he had left. I just think he hoped that somehow he'd get better, but there was nothing anyone could do.

He came to see me play for Wales A against New Zealand at the Millennium Stadium not long before he died and the enjoyment on his face told the whole story. That was a difficult and emotional day, but it meant so much to see him smiling.

He spent the last couple weeks of his life in the Cottage Hospital in Pontypridd and, towards the end, he was in a coma. It was quite peaceful the way he went in the end and we were all there with him.

From the day he was diagnosed to when he passed away in December 2000, it was just three months. To see him decline so rapidly was so hard to take. Craig was more than a brother to me, he was my best friend, and I still miss him so much today. When my son was born in August 2006, we christened him Corey Craig in his uncle's memory. It was just a nice little touch to try and remember Craig by and I always will.

When he died, it was a slap across the face for me and a real wake-up call, because until then everything had gone smoothly. I'd been kind of living in my own little world, moaning about the pettiest little things, and I suppose I was a bit selfish. All of a sudden, reality hit me hard.

I realised that I'd been taking too many things for granted and not really appreciating how lucky I was to have my health and the opportunities I had. You know your playing career is short, people are always harping on about that, but you don't realise just how short life can be as well. Losing Craig hammered home to me that you've got to make the most of everything you've got.

It changed me in a lot of ways and I probably became a stronger person as a result. It made me a lot more determined and spurred me on to make the most of my opportunities and really to make the most of every minute. I trained like never before and worked that much harder.

The easy thing to do would have been to have felt sorry for myself and let things slide. And I'll admit there were days after Craig passed away when I was thinking, 'What's the point, it's only a game?' But I know he wouldn't have wanted me to think like that and I drew strength from him.

I also wanted to achieve something to give my parents something to take their minds off their loss, because I could see how much they were hurting. So I threw everything into it and, six months later, I found myself on the British Lions tour of Australia. I think that helped the family a lot. I know it helped me. From the moment I was selected, I decided to dedicate that trip to Craig, because he had been the one to give me the strength to carry on.

Someone else who has been a constant source of strength and support to me is my wife, Sam. We've known each other since we were twelve, when we were put in the same class in our first year at Coed-y-Lan Comprehensive. She was from Maesycoed, I was from Graigwen, and she was just one of the girls in the class. But over the years we became friends and we started going out when I was in the sixth form. Fifteen years later we're still together and we've got two kids now. I guess it's the genuine childhood sweetheart story.

At first when she started seeing me, when we were seventeen, I was working as a milkman. I used to do the milk round before going to school and I was just playing for Ponty Youth. She had no idea what was ahead of her with the rugby. A lot is asked of a rugby player's wife or partner, especially when there are kids involved, because you are away so much.

Our daughter, Mia, was born in January 2003 during a very difficult time. It was our first child and it was the era when Steve Hansen was the Wales coach and the players had to stay at the team-base at the Vale of Glamorgan hotel pretty much constantly. As hard as it was for me, it was probably doubly hard for Sam.

Looking back, she has been unbelievable putting up with it all and I owe her so much. She was a tower of strength for me when Craig passed away and then again four years later when that same terrible illness claimed my mother.

It was in January 2005 when my mum came over to our house in Pontypridd and said she had a lump on her neck and that she was going to get it checked out. We never thought anything of it. But then, when we went up with her to the hospital, they said she had cancer. And it was the old infamous words of: 'It's treatable, but it's not curable.' It's the worst thing you can possibly hear. She was only forty-seven and, coming after what had happened to Craig, it just seemed so unfair and so cruel.

The next couple of months were surreal. On the rugby pitch it was the happiest time of my life, because Wales won the Grand Slam and I was named player of the Six Nations. But on the other hand it was really tough seeing my mother so ill. I was taking her back and forth to Velindre Hospital in Cardiff for chemotherapy and the treatment was really taking its toll on her.

The one positive thing is that at least I know the rugby took her mind off the disease. She came to the England game at the Millennium Stadium when I won my fiftieth cap and she was there for the Grand Slam-clinching match against Ireland, too. It meant so much to me that she was there for those games and the England match in particular was very emotional, because it came only a few weeks after she'd been diagnosed. I had a letter from one of her friends after she died saying that when I led the Welsh team out that day to mark my fiftieth appearance, my mother said it was the proudest she'd ever been. That's something I'll always keep with me.

After the Six Nations, I was selected for the Lions tour to New Zealand and she wanted to go out there to watch me play. But, after talking with the doctors, it was decided that it would have been a long old trip and too difficult for her. There was never any thought of me not going on the tour. She wouldn't have stood for that. She would have forced me to go.

As soon as I came back, myself and Sam took her to Florida for two weeks, along with our daughter Mia, who was two at the time. That was when I really started to notice how much she was deteriorating. There were a few times out there where she really struggled.

When we got back, she steadily got worse and worse and that was when Sam and I decided to get married. We are both similar in that we just kind of go with things and we'd just never got round to arranging a wedding. But with my mother being so ill, we really wanted to get married while she could be there to see too.

We arranged that wedding in two weeks from start to

finish, which just shows how amazing Sam is. We rang round the immediate family to ask if they could make a date in two weeks time, in mid-September, and we went onto a website called Whirlwind Weddings.

You wouldn't think it was possible to get everything sorted in that short a time, but it turned out to be awesome. Even if I'd have had two years to plan it, it couldn't have been any better. It was at a stately home in Somerset, called St Audrie's, with our fifty closest family and friends.

You see people plan their weddings for two or three years, change their minds and have all these arguments, but we didn't have a chance for any of that. Once we made the decision we had to stick by it. It was such a stressful two weeks to get it all done in time, but it was definitely worth it. It was just a fantastic day and I know my mother said that as well. In one way, it was such a sad time because we all knew she didn't have long left, but it meant so much to see her happy with all her family around her on such a special occasion.

In the last couple of weeks of her life she was in Velindre and they were awesome to her down there. When you see what the nurses go through there, I don't know how they do it. It is amazing to me and I really take my hat off to them. What we went through, they witness every single day. They make me feel very humble. Cancer is one of the most awful things anyone can go through, but they do everything they can to make it that bit more bearable.

They are so supportive of the families and you never felt like you were overstaying your visit. They would go out of their way to help you. I'll always be grateful for what they did for my mother and for us as a family and I do whatever I can to try and help out with fund-raising for the hospital.

The day my mother died was probably the worst day of my life. It was 26 October and I was out in France with the Cardiff Blues for a Heineken Cup game against Perpignan. I'd been reluctant to go, because I knew how ill she was and wanted to be with her. I'd been at her side the whole way through. But she wanted me to play and, in the end, we both decided I should go.

Then, on the morning of the match, I had a call from her doctor to say she had deteriorated and I was asked if there was any chance I could get back home. So I spoke to Dai Young, the Blues coach, and told him I had to go. He was superb about it and the chairman Peter Thomas was even on about hiring a private jet to get me back. Then I had another phone call from the doctor to say it was fine and that I didn't need to come back. But, an hour and a half later, I had a call from my mother's sister, Karen, to say she'd passed away. It was such a tough thing for Karen to have to tell me and it was a really hard call to take.

Then it was a case of getting home. That turned out to be the longest journey of my life. I had to get a taxi from Perpignan to Toulouse airport, which is like an hour and a half's drive, and then it was a flight from Toulouse to Birmingham. I've travelled twenty-seven hours to New Zealand but, trust me, this felt a lot longer. It was just a terrible journey. I was so glad to see my two best friends, Robbie and Jamie, waiting for me at Birmingham airport to drive me home.

The following week, Wales were playing the All Blacks in Cardiff and obviously I withdrew from that match. The Welsh boys wore black armbands during the game in memory of my mother and that meant a hell of a lot to me. It was a really nice touch and a huge thing for them to have done. Watching the game at home and seeing the boys come out wearing the armbands was a very emotional moment.

When I look back at 2005, it seems so strange. It brought me everything I wanted in my rugby career yet, off the field, I also went through the worst time in my life. It's hard to put into words just how much my mother did for me and just how big a part she played in my life. Support-wise she was unbelievable. She was never one of those pushy parents, but from the moment I started playing rugby she used to love to come and watch me play. If I ever needed anything, she'd go out of her way to get it for me. I never wanted for anything. When you are younger, you don't really appreciate what other people have done for you to get you where you are. It's only when you get older you realise the sacrifices they must have made.

Losing both Craig and my mother has had a huge effect on the way I approach life and the people around me. It makes you live life and I treat every day now as a precious commodity. You appreciate things more and the people in your life, because you see how easily things can get taken away. I cherish every moment I get to spend with my two children, and the desire to spend as much time with them as possible was a big factor in deciding to retire from Test rugby. Having kids is the best thing that's ever happened to me and I want to be there for them as much as I can.

The losses I've suffered have also helped me put rugby in its proper perspective. At the end of the day, it is just a game; it's not life and death. If I make a mistake now I don't worry about it, I just make sure I put it right. It's made me realise worse things than dropping a pass or missing a tackle can happen to you.

I think that sense of perspective has actually helped me as a player, because it's kept my feet on the ground and stopped me getting too wrapped up in things. It makes you realise that family is everything and that everything you do is ultimately for them.

Yes, rugby matters, but life matters more.

## chapter 3

# the valley commandos

It didn't take long for me to realise what life with Pontypridd was going to be like.

I was already part of the youth team set-up at Sardis Road and there was a good crack with those boys. But when I moved up to the senior side, it was like entering a different world.

I'll never forget my first game for the club. I was only eighteen and still at school when they asked me to go on a trip up north to play Waterloo in October 1993. I remember we had to turn up at Sardis early in the morning for the bus drive up to Liverpool and there were all these seasoned players there like Phil John, Nigel Bezani and Steele Lewis. I was absolutely scared stiff.

Then, as soon as I got on the bus, the first thing that happened was someone put a can of lager in my hand – at 8 o'clock in the morning! I thought: 'Oh my God, here we go.'

About an hour into the journey, I had to go to the back

of the bus to use the toilet and I remember Phil John – a larger-than-life hooker who was never short of a word – saying, 'Who the hell are you?' That was my introduction to it all.

It was still in the amateur days back then and there was a real drinking culture in Welsh rugby. For that Waterloo trip, we went up on the Thursday, drank all day and all night and then played the game on the Friday afternoon. When it came to the match, the boys really wanted to win and switched on. But, looking back, the preparation for it was unbelievable.

For me, the experience was all the more bizarre because the scrum-half was Paul John, a top-quality player who went on to win a number of caps for Wales. I was in the sixth form at Coed-y-Lan Comprehensive at the time and Paul was my PE teacher. That made it even worse in a way. To go on a rugby trip and have your teacher there as a team-mate was really strange.

So it was an eye-opening weekend for me in a lot of ways and a real initiation. As an eighteen-year-old it was such an experience. I learned a hell of a lot on that trip and it still sticks in my mind to this day.

You had all the main men there, huge characters like Phil John, or 'Ghurka' as he was known to everyone, 'Baz' Bezani and the third member of the front-row union, Neil Eynon: you just couldn't stay in your shell with people like that about.

I followed that up just over a year later with a trip to Dundee, this time on an international weekend. That was pretty much the same thing, with the drink flowing from start to finish and a game of rugby fitted in somewhere

*Top left*: Season's Greetings: Me and my grandfather on Christmas Day in the early 80s with me proudly wearing my new Liverpool shirt.

*Above*: Big Brother: Enjoying Christmas Day with my younger brother Craig.

*Top right*: Birthday boy, aged four. What was my mother thinking dressing me like this?

*Right*: Trophy time – celebrating victory with Pontydun Mini Rugby U12s in the Marlow Tournament.

*Top*: Reluctant captain. Handed the reins for the first time with the Pontydun U10s, coached by Jack Bayliss (far right).

*Above*: Muddy memory: My first ever game on Cardiff Arms Park for East Wales U11 vs West Wales.

*Bottom right*: A night out with the boys in my Pontypridd Youth Days.

There was a real one-for-all, all-for-one spirit at Pontypridd and I am very grateful for having started my career in such a close-knit team.

*Top left*: Crashing into Llanelli's Iwan Jones in April 1998.

*Top right*: Against Bonymaen, May 1999.

*Middle*: Putting a stop to Scott Gibbs in a match against Swansea, May 1998.

*Bottom left*: Breaking from Llanelli's Rupert Moon to score a try in September 1998.

In action for Pontypridd against Stade Français in early 1999.

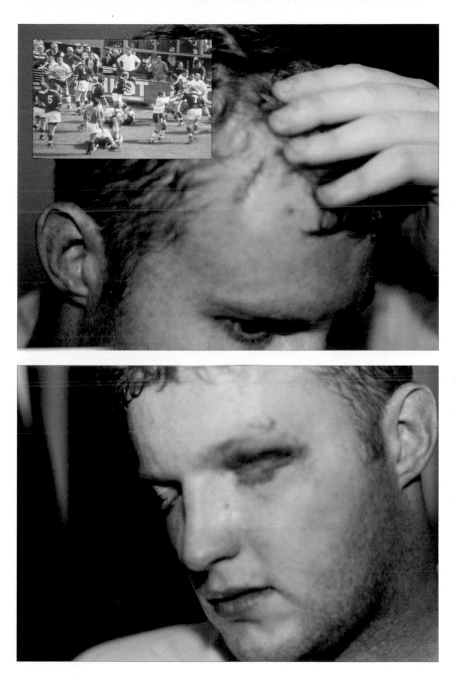

My wounds sustained at the infamous Battle of Brive. The match is remembered for the brawl (*inset*), but it was a superb game of rugby.

It wasn't an easy decision moving from Ponty to Cardiff, but I knew that if I wanted to further my career, it was the best thing to do.

*Top*: Matches against the team who'd nurtured me for six years were always a challenge. Here I am being taken down by Michael Owen and Nick Kelly.

*Bottom*: I will be able to look back on my time at Cardiff with great fondness – there's no feeling to compare with scoring the winning try for the team who has given you so much.

*Top*: Making for the line against Glasgow.

*Bottom*: Photographer Huw Evans has been taking shots of me on the pitch ever since I was in youth rugby. This one captures the moment I feed the ball out during a Swansea v Cardiff game, watched by Iestyn Harris and Scott Gibbs.

A lot of my success is down to the guys who do so much off the pitch.

*Top left*: Steve Hansen and Scott Johnson really pushed us to develop ourselves as a tightly-knit team, but encouraged a great balance between training and time off, too.

*Top right*: Mark Davies is a class physio, full of stories and a great guy to be on tour with.

*Above*: Fitness coach Andrew Hore was a hard taskmaster but no one can deny that his techniques got results.

*Bottom right*: Pictured presenting a shirt to fellow openside flanker Prince William following the Six Nations game against Ireland in February 2007.

© *Huw Evans*

along the way. You wonder now how you managed to do it. There's no way you could get away with it these days.

But the point was we played hard, but we worked hard as well. That was just the kind of character and attitude that was there at the time.

When I compare those days to what happens now, it just seems like another world. After a game now, whether it be for the Cardiff Blues or for Wales, you often have a pool recovery session and there's a big emphasis on taking the right kind of fluids on board. With Ponty, when I started out, the emphasis was on refuelling of a different kind. It would be a quick shower, put some tidy clothes on and get into the clubhouse as fast as you can. It's amazing how far things have come in such a short space of time.

I used to go out a fair bit when I was younger, just with friends, but the drinking with the Ponty boys was on a different level to anything I'd experienced before. You would play a game at 2.30pm on a Saturday afternoon and you'd spend all night in the clubhouse. I can even remember some nights you'd stay there until it got light the next morning. That was just the culture there was at the time.

I didn't know how I was going to cope to start off with, but you quickly got into the swing of things and I didn't do too badly! Like I say, that was the culture in Welsh rugby at the time, but I think it was even more extreme at Ponty.

We all used to socialise together and we liked to have a good time. You would never get away with the sort of things we got up to now, but the thing was we were really successful on the field. It was a brilliant place to be and a great bunch of boys to be around.

There was a real one-for-all, all-for-one spirit and you knew if you went into battle, your mates would be right behind you. That led to us picking up the nickname of the 'Valley Commandos'.

Every club probably had a really good spirit, but Ponty just seemed that to be that bit different. It was such a close-knit thing we had going there.

In a way that might seem a bit strange, because there was such a mixture of people there. You obviously had the local valleys boys, like Baz from Tylorstown, Ghurka from Quakers Yard and Steele 'Stella' Lewis from Gilfach Goch. But you also had the Cardiff crew there as well, with the likes of Matthew Lloyd, Matthew De Maid, Jonathan Evans, Crispin Cormack and Simon Enoch.

You had roofers and scaffolders playing alongside Cambridge University graduates and teachers, but somehow it all gelled together and everyone got on really, really well. That kind of mix helped with the banter and there was no shortage of that around the place.

It's difficult to say who the maddest of the lot were, but Ghurka and his front-row pal Eynon were right up there as real characters. They would just bounce off each other and when the mickey-taking and the banter started, they were just head and shoulders above everyone else.

They were the two that really ran the show, along with Baz, Stella and Dale McIntosh, our hard-as-nails No. 8 from New Zealand. They were the main men and, to be honest, I was scared stiff of them when I first joined the squad.

With guys like Dale and Stella, their reputations went

before them, and you didn't take any liberties. Before you actually got in with them, it was a daunting place to be, but it was really character building for a young kid. It could either make you or break you. You could either shy away from it or, if they accepted you, then you were made. Luckily, I managed to fit in pretty well.

The coaches throughout my time with the first-team were Dennis John and Lynn Howells, who both went on to coach Wales in different capacities. I will be forever grateful to those two, because they gave me my first opportunity. They gave me a chance when I was young and I learned a hell of a lot from them.

I was pretty scared of them when I first turned up, though. They told it like it was and there was no messing about with them. I can still remember Dennis talking to me in front of everyone at training one night a couple of days before we played Ebbw Vale who, at the time, had an outstanding scrum-half called Dai Llewellyn.

He warned me that Llewellyn would make me look like a little boy if I wasn't totally switched on. It was a bit of a shock to the system at the time to be talked to like that in front of all the other players, but it got my attention and it paid off.

Looking back, it was good that Dennis and Lynn didn't mollycoddle you just because you were a youngster. I think perhaps young players now are mollycoddled a little bit too much. But those two guys were great coaches and they definitely helped in my development.

Someone else who really helped me a lot when I first broke into the team was Neil Jenkins. Neil was Mr Ponty at the time. He was a superstar, the main man in Wales, but it didn't change him as a person one bit. He still remained the same down-to-earth guy and he had time for everyone.

I was just a nineteen-year-old kid coming out of youth, but he used to take me down to Sardis and train with me, just me and him, doing extra fitness sessions. That meant a hell of a lot and I've got the utmost respect for the guy. His dedication and commitment to the game were second to none and he deserved everything he achieved during his career.

He came in for a lot of really unfair criticism at times in the mid-1990s when Wales were going through some tough times and the way he kept on going and rose above the flak was a testament to his character.

At Ponty, everything revolved around him in terms of the way we played as a team. He called the shots at fly-half, dictated the gameplan and was a real match-winner. Some people saw him as just a kicker, but he was so much more than that. He had wonderful passing ability and superb vision and he was the catalyst of the high-tempo game we played. That was the kind of rugby he wanted to play and it really suited us as a team. In a way, I think it was quite ahead of its time.

When I joined the set-up, the club had been doing well for a couple of years before that but hadn't managed to pick up any silverware. They had come close in the league and lost the 1995 Welsh Cup final to Swansea. This led to them picking up the unwanted label as the 'nearly men'.

But in May 1996 they finally rid themselves of that mantle when they beat Neath at the National Stadium in Cardiff to win the Welsh Cup for the first time. It was a great achievement for the club and, as a Ponty boy, I was delighted, but I hadn't been involved in the final myself, as I was still on the fringes of the squad. I had three really good open-sides above me in Richie Collins, Kingsley Jones and Phil Thomas, so there was a lot of competition for places. But seeing the team pick up the trophy made me all the more determined to get into the side and share in a moment like that myself.

As it turned out, I didn't have to wait too long. The following season we went on to win the league and this time I was to share in the success. I played in more or less every game during that season and it was a fantastic experience. It stands out as a really good memory and a great way to have started off my career.

At home, we put thirty or forty points on most sides and played in front of full houses virtually every week. The whole town was buzzing and there was a great atmosphere around the place. We played some fantastic rugby that season and thoroughly deserved to win the title.

We had a really good mix of youngsters, like Kevin Morgan, Gareth Wyatt and myself who were just starting out, another group of guys in their mid-twenties, plus boys coming towards the end of their careers, like Ghurka and Stella.

There was a good balance to the team as well. We had pace and flair behind, but we also had the grunt up front, while Paul John and Neil held it all together at half-back. They had been playing together since they were in Llantwit Fardre Under-8s, where they had been coached by Paul's father Dennis. Fifteen years on, they knew each other's game inside out and Dennis was still holding the reins.

Outside them were the Lewis brothers, Steele and Jason, who were brilliant centres and definitely underrated. I can remember them coming up against more-vaunted partnerships like Scott Gibbs and Mark Taylor at Swansea, and they would have the better of them on numerous occasions.

We had another outstanding double-act in the second row, where Greg Prosser and Mark Rowley were as good a club pairing as there was in Wales, and from my perspective as a flanker it was just a joy to play behind the front five we had back then.

I've also got to make a quick mention of Phil Ford, the brother of Cardiff and Wales winger Steve, who came down from rugby league. Everyone looked at us and said 'What are you signing him for?', but he was brilliant for us that year.

He hadn't played that much union and his famous quote was 'Keep me out of those gangs'. Gangs is what he used to call rucks! But he did a great job for us and he used to look after us off the field as well. He used to run the Carpenters Arms in Cardiff and that became a regular haunt of ours.

We clinched the title with a couple of games to spare by winning at Bridgend, but the WRU didn't have a trophy for us. It was disappointing, but it was typical of the times really. That was how professional it was in those days.

After the game at Bridgend, it was straight back to the club and that was awesome. It really stands out as a brilliant memory. Between the stand and the clubhouse at

Sardis, there's an open area and that was just jam-packed with supporters. When we got off the bus, we were cheered and clapped in and, when you are twenty-one, that's something really special. Being from Ponty and growing up in the town, it meant all the more to me and I know Kevin Morgan and Gareth Wyatt felt the same.

That season we also had a pretty memorable campaign in Europe. We played Bath at Sardis Road and beat them and it was the best atmosphere I'd ever experienced at the ground. Bath were the biggest club in Britain at the time and for us, a valleys' side, to turn them over was a huge thing.

It's a game that will always be remembered for Dale McIntosh's huge hits on the future England coach Andy Robinson. He smashed Robinson twice and all you could hear echoing around the ground was the crowd chanting Dale's nickname 'Chief'.

After the game, he was the centre of attention with the media and they all wanted to know where his nickname came from. They presumed it was because he was like some kind of Maori chief and I'm sure he'd like that to be the reason. But the truth was it was because he looked like the character called The Chief from the film *One Flew Over the Cuckoo's Nest*. One thing there was no confusion over, though, was just how much the fans loved him.

He epitomised Ponty at the time and he's gone on to become a Sardis Road legend. He may be a Kiwi by birth, but he's been long-since adopted as one of the valleys' favourite sons.

He was a huge influence on me when I was starting out,

especially with him being a No. 8 and me a seven. I used to change next to him in the dressing room and when you run out with someone like that, who has no fear of anyone, it makes a huge difference. The guy just had the heart of a lion and didn't know the meaning of taking a backward step.

An injury that would keep most people out for six weeks, he'd be back from in two. He was quite inspirational for me as a youngster and that game against Bath really epitomised what he was about. I wouldn't say he won the game on his own, but he had a massive influence on it. The hits he put in just lifted everyone in our team and knocked a dent in theirs.

In the end, we just failed to qualify from our group, losing unluckily out in Dax, who had the likes of Fabien Pelous and Olivier Magne in their ranks at the time, but it was all part of a truly memorable season.

Those were special days at Ponty and there was a tremendous atmosphere at our home games. You more or less knew 90 percent of the crowd. All your mates would go, all your family would go and all the people who lived in the same street with you would be there as well.

I was living in Ponty back then and it was a special time. You'd go to other grounds and they'd be packed, but the atmosphere wasn't quite the same. You speak to any players from any club that used to go there at the time and they really loved playing there, even if our crowd won us a few games, by swaying refs with decisions you wouldn't normally get.

It's more than eight years now since I left Ponty, but the values I gained there still serve me well today. I wouldn't have achieved half of what I've achieved in the game if I hadn't had that upbringing. It was a special place and a special time.

All of which makes it so sad that there's no professional team based up there any more. It's a crying shame when you consider what a fertile area for rugby talent it is. You only have to look at the Wales Grand Slam team of 2005 to see that. Six of the pack had been involved with Ponty at one time or another – Gethin Jenkins, Mefin Davies, Brent Cockbain, Robert Sidoli, Michael Owen and myself – while you also had Kevin Morgan at full-back.

If you speak to them, they'll all say they had values that were forged in Pontypridd, so it's really sad to see what has happened to rugby in the town since the move to regional rugby.

It's a very difficult situation, because obviously we couldn't sustain nine professional clubs, either financially or in terms of playing resources. It did need to be narrowed down, but I think it is a real shame that the valleys have suffered so badly, especially since the demise of the Celtic Warriors.

If you look at the squad the Warriors had, through bringing together the best players from Ponty and Bridgend, it was immense. But it all ended so unhappily when that region folded after just one season and there are a lot of people still bearing the scars from that whole experience.

It's been left to the Cardiff Blues to pick up the pieces in the valleys and they are trying their best, employing guys like The Chief to develop young talent in the area. I think people are buying into the regional concept a little bit more now, especially the younger generation.

You are always going to get diehards who will vow 'I will never be a Blue' and I can totally understand that because I'm from the area and there's a lot of hurt there. If I wasn't playing the game, I could well be one of those people. But you can't turn the clock back. You've got to move forward. And with that in mind, I'd like to see the Blues play some games up at Ponty. I don't mean a token pre-season fixture or a match against someone like Borders or Connacht, but a big game.

I think you'd be surprised how many people you'd get up there. You might get a few Ponty people going there to support the other side, but I'm sure you'd get a lot coming to shout on the Blues as well. My former Wales team-mate Gareth 'Alfie' Thomas has done a few rugby camps in the valleys and he's been amazed talking to the young kids how much they love the Blues.

They haven't really got that association with the old Ponty side or any of the baggage that comes from the past. They just love rugby and for them the Blues is their region. So in that sense I guess it's about skipping a generation and building for the future.

Then again, you never know. One day, somewhere down the line, they might put a team back in the valleys. The support base is there and so is the talent. So who knows, those special Ponty days might return once more.

# the battle of brive

Of all the days in my rugby career, 13 September 1997 probably stands out as the most extraordinary. It's a date that can be summed up in four words: The Battle of Brive.

That phrase is now part of rugby folklore and much has been said and written over the years about the events on that autumn day in central France. But only those who were actually there know the full story. Well, I was there and I've got the scars to prove it.

I was only twenty-one at the time and was still learning my trade with Pontypridd. We had been crowned Welsh champions the season before and the next target was to conquer Europe. But our Heineken Cup campaign got off to a disappointing start when we lost at home to Bath, who we'd beaten in the previous year's competition. We were immediately up against it and the pressure was on. Now we had to go out to France to face the European champions, Brive.

No one gave us a hope, because all the other sides that had gone out there had got blown away. There was an aura of invincibility about the French sides at the time. You had no chance of going there and getting a result – that was the way of thinking back then. But we were never really ones for conforming or following the script at Ponty. We weren't about to go over there and just lie down. That wasn't in our nature.

All week in the build-up to the game, we'd been stoking ourselves up and getting ready to tackle Brive head on. Our team manager, Eddie Jones, had talked a lot about the need to show some of the old Ponty fire and to get in among the French.

A colourful character with a unique way of expressing himself, Eddie had said it was time for us to cut out the pretty stuff and 'the college-boy rugby' and concentrate on a spot of 'trench warfare'.

Tellingly, he also sent out a clear message to Brive by declaring, 'We've got the bottle for it. We don't get intimidated easily, which is what French sides like to do. They don't give you apples, they give you the swede!' Good old Eddie, he was never short of a word or two.

But that gives you some idea of what our mind-set was like going out there and that just grew in intensity once we actually arrived in the town. I remember just before we left the hotel for the ground, Phil John and Dale 'The Chief' McIntosh asked the coaches to leave us and they kept the boys in there.

What sticks out in my mind is Phil saying how everyone back in the pubs in Ponty would be watching the game on TV and how we mustn't let them down or let ourselves down. I had never seen a side so over-the-top fired-up for a game and I haven't in the decade since. It literally was the old banging the heads against the wall syndrome. It was very much the old school. The boys just couldn't wait to get out there.

At the time, Brive were coached by Laurent Seigne, the former French international prop, and intimidation was a big part of their mentality. They had guys like Philippe Carbonneau, the scrum-half, who was an absolute wind-up merchant, and I was to get to know him quite well over the course of the day.

When the game got under way, it was pretty physical and uncompromising from the outset. There were a few sparky moments as we stood up to them and refused to back off, but after about twenty minutes things really kicked off.

We were pressing on their line and, as they put in a clearance kick, The Chief tackled one of their players. It just all blew up, with two or three of the Brive guys setting on him.

I can remember being the first one in and grabbing his arms to try and pull him away. But that just made matters worse for him, because he couldn't defend himself then and they were hitting him from all sides – he gave me some terrible stick for that afterwards! – and within a matter of seconds everyone was involved in the fight. It became a mass brawl.

We had spoken before the game about what our approach would be in that kind of situation. It wasn't so much a 99 call, like the British Lions had in the 1970s, but we just said if it does kick off, then everyone is in. We weren't going to back down to these guys. So everyone was involved in it. I think even our winger Gareth Wyatt ran in and got a bit of sweat on his jersey.

It seemed like the fight went on forever. It broke up, stopped, then kicked off again. I can remember being in the middle of it in my own private little battle. Luckily I was up against the smallest one there, Carbonneau, but he was quite a tasty little fella. He was renowned as a fiery so-and-so and he was quite quick with his hands.

I think I beat him on points just, but as people often remind me, little Arwel Thomas had dropped him with one punch in the France-Wales game earlier that year. So Arwel's obviously tougher than me!

When the fighting finally stopped, The Chief was red carded along with their flanker Lionel Mallier, but really you could have sent off as many as you wanted. As The Chief walked off, he gave the old thumbs up to the crowd who were giving him the bird and that just wound them up even more.

Looking back, I think it all went off because we stood up to Brive. They were schoolyard bullies and they probably expected to have an easy ride, which is what they usually got when sides went out there. But I remember all week the talk in our camp had been that, whatever happens, we had to front up to them. That's what we did and they didn't like it.

Everyone remembers the match for the fighting and that's understandable. But what is sometimes overlooked is the fact that the actual game itself was superb. Both sides played rugby and it was back and forth from one end to the other.

At one point it looked as though they were out of sight, but then Dafydd James scored a brilliant try and when I chipped ahead for Kevin Morgan to touch down we were ahead and on course for a famous win. But then, right at the death, they were awarded a pushover try to give them a 32–31 victory.

It's more than ten years on now, but it still rankles, because it was never a try. There was so much frustration among us afterwards. It would have been such an historic victory because they were European champions and we would have been the first Welsh team to win in France in the competition. But, of course, while the match itself may have been eventful enough, it's what happened afterwards that has really acquired the Battle of Brive legendary status.

It's different nowadays, because for most European trips you fly straight back home after the game. But in those days, especially at Ponty, we'd make a good weekend of it. We had loads of travelling support with us and it was usually a good-natured party atmosphere. This time, however, the atmosphere was to get distinctly hot – red-hot in fact.

My memory of the events is that a couple of the Brive players invited us to go for a drink at a bar in the town centre – a place called Le Bar Toulzac. I think they had a bit of respect for us because we'd fronted up to them in the game, so they said come along and we'll have a good drink together.

The Toulzac was quite a small place, a kind of long, narrow bar. I can remember being in there talking to David Venditti, their winger, and then later on sitting with

Matthew De Maid, Jonathan Evans and Jason Lewis. Generally, if I was out, I was always with Jason because we were good mates.

There didn't seem to be any problem at all, but then, all of a sudden, you could see this fracas developing in the corner and it all kind of kicked off over there.

Later, I found out that Carbonneau and Phil John were the two involved at the start of it. Phil thought Carbonneau was winding him up and Phil is never one to take a backward step, so there was a bit of aggro between them. That was sort of brought under control after a bit and we all decided it was best to leave.

But then, just as we were leaving, a bottle was thrown at us from where the Brive players were standing and it caught Jason on the head. That was it. That was the signal for all hell to break loose.

After that, it was just like you see in the Wild West films. There were chairs flying through the air and smashing into the shorts bottles behind the bar as the barman dived for cover. It was just chaos in there. The place was smashed to bits. I don't know what the cost was, but it must have been a fair bit.

The fighting must have gone on for five or ten minutes, much longer than the brawl on the field. Eventually the police arrived and just basically cleaned the place out, handing out a bit of treatment to the boys as they did so.

I remember coming out with blood pouring down my face and down the back of my head from two separate gashes. I'm not sure if that was from the police with their batons or from the chairs that were being thrown. It was just that kind of melee.

Our club doctor, Dave Pemberton, who went on to work with Wales, had to take me back to the hotel to get me stitched up. I'm lucky the scars have healed up a bit now as at the time some of them were pretty wide.

When we got back to the hotel, we were all sitting in the bar and chatting and kind of laughing about it all, because the adrenaline was still flowing. Apparently a few cars pulled up outside with the Brive boys and other locals in, but luckily it was left there.

We all thought that was the end of it, but that proved anything but the case.

I was rooming with Jason Lewis and I remember him waking me up the next morning and saying there were police outside the hotel. Then, all of a sudden, Jason and I got pulled in for questioning by the Gendarme, along with Jason's brother Steel, Phil John, Andre Barnard and The Chief.

Some of the Brive players had made a complaint and we were the ones that got picked out. It didn't make much sense, because The Chief had had very little to do with the fight in the night because he'd got out of the place early on.

What we later found out was apparently they had just picked out boys they recognised from the game and who they could remember. That was the whole crux of it: they picked us out by our numbers and there must have been some confusion over them. It all led to Andre, our replacement centre, being wrongly identified.

Anyway, all six of us had to go down to the police station to get questioned and I can tell you I was scared that Sunday morning.

I was only twenty-one and I'd never been involved with the police or anything like that before. To be sat there in a police station in a foreign country, not being able to speak the language and not knowing what was going to happen to me was a frightening experience.

You knew damage had been done to the bar and you could tell the French were being biased and were trying to exaggerate the things that you had done. Being questioned by those policemen was one of the scariest times of my life.

Luckily, myself and the Lewis brothers were released, but they kept the other three boys out there and they had to stay over in France for an extra night.

It was a huge relief for me to be able to go home, but that wasn't entirely the last I heard of the incident. I was still receiving letters summoning me out there six or seven years later as the result of some random guy who wanted compensation from me because he claimed he'd had to miss work through his injuries.

Fortunately, it's never affected me going back to France, but there were ramifications for The Chief, Phil and Andre, who weren't allowed back to Brive for a quarter-final play-off six weeks later. And Ponty were fined £30,000 – £15,000 of that amount suspended – by the competition organisers for our part in the mass brawl during the game.

Looking back, it was an experience which, if anything, made us tighter as a group.

You can't condone what went on, either on or off the field. That should never happen. But it was a case of a load of guys sticking up for each other and looking after their mates.

After the game, the Brive coach Seigne called us 'semi-civilised animals', which was rich given some of the things his players got up to. One of the main players on their side, Carbonneau, was put up before the French media, along with the centre Christophe Lamaison, for them to photograph their bruised faces. Ponty responded by taking pictures of me and issuing them to the press; I certainly looked a bit of state.

Two weeks later, the sides met in a re-match at Sardis Road. Brive had said they didn't want to come to Ponty, but were ordered to fulfil the fixture. Not that they stayed in town too long, shooting off straight after an incident-free draw.

As fate would have it, we were drawn to face each other again in a play-off, which meant a return to Brive. With The Chief, Phil and Andre barred from the region, it was always going to be a tough ask for us, but it proved another classic encounter as we came from behind to take the lead only to lose out to another dodgy try.

For everything unsavoury that happened along the way, those three games against Brive stand out as real highlights of my career and show what a wonderful competition the Heineken Cup is. It's a tournament I feel a lot of affinity with, because we both kind of started out at the same time.

It was launched in the 1995–96 campaign and that was really my first season as a full-time member of the Ponty squad. Over the years, it's kind of been a constant companion and it's given me some great memories along the way.

When I think of some of the teams I've played against

in the competition, it's like a Who's Who of European rugby. Just look at the list: Toulouse, Munster, Leicester, Stade Francais, Ulster, Biarritz, Northampton, Leinster, Bath and not forgetting our old friends from Brive.

Travelling around Europe and taking on these kind of teams has been a fantastic experience and a real rugby education. There's no doubt in my mind that the Heineken Cup has been one of the great successes of the professional era and it's just grown in stature year after year.

You ask any of the Welsh boys and they'll tell you how much they look forward to playing in it. As soon as the fixtures come out each season, the first thing you do is check out your European games. It's the closest you can get to Test rugby in terms of intensity and playing standards and some of the games are like mini-internationals.

I'd love to get my hands on the trophy before I hang up my boots and that remains a definite ambition, although I realise time is running out. So far, the best I've done is three quarter-final appearances, one for Ponty and two for Cardiff. Unfortunately, all three have been days to forget.

The first of those came the year after Brive, when Ponty finally reached the last eight. But, to be honest, we probably didn't play as well that season as we had in the previous two when we'd missed out.

It was the year the English clubs boycotted Europe and there was no Cardiff or Swansea either, because they were in exile playing Anglo-Welsh rebel matches. So, on paper, qualifying for the quarter-finals was a lot easier, with two teams going through from each of the four groups. But we still made hard work of it, only just managing to squeeze through as our group's runner-up. We also found ourselves involved in another off-the-field altercation along the way – and once again in France.

This followed our game away to the eventual group winners Colomiers. After the game, there was a bit of an incident at a nightclub in nearby Toulouse, which saw a window getting smashed. It was nothing compared to what had happened in Brive, but we ended up getting fined £5,000 as a club and there were threats that we could be expelled from Europe if there were any more unwelcome incidents.

The competition organisers must have been anxious when we were drawn away to French club Stade Francais in the quarter-finals. But the only damage done that weekend just before Christmas 1998 was to our pride. After working so hard for so long to get to the quarter-finals, it proved a huge anti-climax as we were smashed 71–14 out in Paris.

Stade were sensational that day, but it was a real wake-up call for us about our fitness levels and the strength of our squad. As soon as Neil Jenkins went off injured, we just fell to pieces.

A lot of players were coming to the end of their careers at the time and the squad needed freshening up. I felt if we could sign two or three big players, especially in the tight five, then we could compete, because our back row was good and the back line was awesome.

But Ponty didn't have the financial clout to get those players in and they weren't prepared to go beyond their means. That was totally understandable, but you could see that we were not going to get much further as a side. So, for the first time, the unthinkable began to enter my mind and I wondered whether it might be time to move on to pastures new.

## chapter 5

# blue (and black) is the colour

It was always going to be a big wrench to leave Pontypridd. It was my hometown club, I'd been there since I was sixteen and I'd never really wanted to play for anyone else.

I'd made some great friends there and had some fantastic times. Even though I sensed things were coming towards the end of an era during that 1998–99 season, I wasn't particularly unhappy.

But then, in February 1999, I was approached by Cardiff. I spoke to a few people I respected and they said it wouldn't harm me to go and speak to them. So I met up with their coach Terry Holmes and chief executive Gareth Davies at the Friendly Hotel on the outskirts of Cardiff. I didn't have an agent at the time. I just went down there on my own and they offered me a contract. It was as simple as that.

Financially, Cardiff were offering me way more than Ponty and when you are a young kid that makes you think. On top of that, you had to be impressed by the squad they were assembling, with the likes of Rob Howley, Gareth Thomas, Dai Young and Jonathan Humphreys, who were all key men in the Welsh squad, already on board and with plans to bring in other big names as well. So I agreed to sign. I just thought it was too good an opportunity to miss.

But then I changed my mind.

Ponty were promising they were going to do this and that and saying they were going to bring players in, so I decided to stay. The club had done a lot for me over the years and I felt I had to give them a chance if they were genuine about strengthening the squad.

But the turning point for me came with what happened over Peter Rogers. Ponty were intending to sign him from London Irish and Peter was the main man at the time, having made a huge impact since coming into the Wales team earlier that year to prop up the scrum. If Ponty were intending to sign him, it meant they had to mean business.

But when I spoke to Peter about it, he told me they hadn't offered him anything and that he wasn't coming. It made me think they weren't really going forward at all and that they genuinely lacked ambition.

I remember ringing up the Wales fitness coach Steve Black and asking his advice, because he was hugely respected by the boys. It wasn't a case of him sending me to Cardiff, but he had an insight into Welsh rugby and he said it would probably be better for my career if I went down there. So that was it, my mind was made up. I was off to the Arms Park.

I knew from speaking to a few of the other Wales boys

at Ponty that they were thinking of leaving as well and, in the end, Kevin Morgan, Dafydd James and even 'Mr Ponty' Neil Jenkins all moved on that summer, with Jenks joining me at the Arms Park.

But I was actually the first one to decide to go and I had to take a fair bit of stick, what with being a Ponty lad and going to their arch-rivals Cardiff as well. If I had gone across the bridge to England it wouldn't have been so bad. Bath were interested at the time and if I'd gone there or to Gloucester maybe it wouldn't have been such a major thing.

But the Blue & Blacks were the Ponty fans' sworn enemies and, predictably, my move didn't go down too well with the Sardis Road faithful. Yet, while I did get a bit of stick, what I really encountered more than anything was people telling me that going to Cardiff would ruin me as a player.

I remember people stopping me in the street in Ponty and saying, 'You don't want to go down there, you'll just end up sitting on the bench and you'll go backwards.' People said I was just going down there for the money and that I'd finish up like all the other players they had wasted down the years. To be fair, there had been a history of players moving to Cardiff and then failing to live up to their potential and everyone in Ponty was saying, 'They are going to ruin you just the same.'

But, from day one, I was adamant that wasn't going to happen to me. That was the whole goal in my head. I wanted to prove so many people wrong and I was determined to be successful.

The move came at a time in my career when I could

quite easily have gone backwards. I wasn't really a regular in the Welsh side under Graham Henry and I knew that if things didn't go well at the Arms Park, there was a possibility I could drop out of the squad altogether.

But I wasn't going to be a failure. I was totally single-minded on that. So when I was voted player of the year in my first season at the club it meant a hell of a lot to me. And nine years and seventy-odd caps further down the line, I'd like to think the move to Cardiff didn't turn out too badly.

Yet although my own career may have blossomed during that time, I do feel an enormous sense of frustration that we haven't achieved the level of success as a team I'd hoped for when I first joined the club.

A big reason for moving to the capital was a desire to get my hands on some silverware and, in my very first season with the club, I did just that when we won the Welsh-Scottish League title.

I wasn't quite as heavily involved in that success as I had been when Ponty had won the league because it was a World Cup season and the Wales players only came in for the second half of the campaign. But it was still great to pick up a trophy and I hoped it would be the first of many. Sadly, that wasn't to be the case.

Looking back, we really should have achieved more than we did during my early years with the club, especially in the 2000–01 season. If you look at that team on paper, it should have been one of *the* great Welsh sides.

You rattle off the names and it reads like a Who's Who of Welsh rugby from the time – Rob Howley, Neil Jenkins, Gareth Thomas, Dai Young, Craig Quinnell,

Emyr Lewis, plus exciting young backs like Rhys Williams, Jamie Robinson and Craig Morgan. When you talk about it with any of the boys now, they say: 'My God, were you all really there together?'

You also had the overseas contingent, with that great South African centre Pieter Muller and two outstanding Canadian forwards in Dan Baugh and John Tait.

Sometimes I come across the team photo in the clubhouse and, when you look at the talent there, you think we really should have done better. And 2001 was the year. It was the season we should have conquered Europe.

Not that our Heineken Cup campaign got off to the best start that season: we lost our opening game away to Ulster in October 2000. But we got things back on track by beating Toulouse 26–17 at the Arms Park, with Neil Jenkins scoring twenty-one points, and then it was back-to-back games against Saracens, beginning with a trip to Vicarage Road.

At the time, Sarries were really flying. They had international stars like Thomas Castaignede, Richard Hill, Danny Grewcock, Scott Murray, Kyran Bracken, Dan Luger and Paul Wallace in their ranks and they were head and shoulders above anyone else in the English Premiership. But we just took them apart.

That game stands out as one of the highlights of my Cardiff career and one of the best performances I've been involved with at any level.

English rugby at the time was seen as being leagues above Welsh rugby. So, for us to go up there, as a Welsh club, and turn over the top English side was something special.

It was a really feisty game, with five players being sin-binned, but we stood up to them and played some fantastic rugby, with Baugh and Muller in particular having outstanding games as we scored four tries to run out 32–23 winners.

After that I think we started to believe among ourselves that we could go on and win the whole tournament; a feeling that became a conviction when we qualified for the quarter-finals with a game to spare after winning the return with Sarries and then thumping Ulster at home as well.

Those two games saw Neil Jenkins at the absolute peak of his powers. He was always a class act, but at that particular point in his career his all-round game was just superb. I would say he was arguably the best player in Britain, if not Europe, at the time.

He scored all our points, landing eight penalties, when we completed the double over Saracens with a 24–14 victory, as hostilities were renewed in a game that saw four more players heading for the bin.

Then, against Ulster, he produced an even better performance. This time he varied his game beautifully, making breaks, throwing dummies, passing superbly off either hand and kicking with perfect precision. He capped his display with a deserved try to finish with twenty-seven points, equalling Cardiff's Heineken Cup record, which had been set by another Pontypridd fly-half product, Lee Jarvis, against Munster in 1997. It was a real masterclass from Neil, but the whole team was firing that night as we ran out 42–16 winners, with Jamie Robinson crossing twice in the centre, and a lot of people were now tipping us as genuine contenders to be European champions.

We lost our last pool game out in Toulouse, always a

tough place to go, which meant we had to go away to Gloucester in the quarters. However, with the side we had, we entered that game with supreme confidence.

But from the moment we ran out at Kingsholm we knew we were in trouble: the pitch was an absolute bog. It was just a quagmire, which suited the way they wanted to play and didn't really suit us, because with the talent we had, our strength was moving the ball out wide and using our backs. We also had a French referee and it's always difficult to get an away win when you've got one of those in charge.

The year before, we had gone to Llanelli for an all-Welsh Heineken Cup quarter-final and lost. On that occasion, we felt we were beaten by the better side on the day and didn't have any qualms with it. But I still feel quite bitter about the Gloucester game, because we felt we didn't really have the fair share of decisions.

Don't get me wrong, Gloucester are a difficult team to beat on their own patch, especially with The Shed screaming them on, and their pack probably outplayed ours that day, with their scrum going particularly well, but we still felt we were on the back foot as a result of a lot of decisions going against us. It's a memory that has left a bitter taste in my mouth.

We took a lot of stick after that defeat, and rightly so, because when you look at the side we had on paper, compared to Gloucester's, then it's a game we should have won. It was probably the beginning of the end for Lynn Howells' reign as coach there as well. Lynn had followed me in moving from Ponty to Cardiff two years earlier to take over from Terry Holmes.

When he first told me he was going there, I just assumed it would be as forwards coach, because that was the job he had done under Dennis John at Sardis. But when he said it was as head coach, I thought it was brilliant: he deserved it for the work he had done at Ponty and alongside Graham Henry with Wales. I respected him for what he'd done for me as a player and I was pleased he was getting the recognition he deserved.

I thought he had done a great job in his first season at Cardiff at a time when all the club's big names were away at the World Cup. He drafted in other players and got the best out of the team, so much so we won the league that year.

But, ultimately, our performances in Europe would be the standard by which he would be judged. That was the Holy Grail for the club at the time and, quite simply, we weren't able to deliver.

We got to two Heineken Cup quarter-finals under Lynn, which would be seen as a success now, but back then, given the side we had, it was deemed a big failure. When a coach has so many big names in the team, it's a no-win situation. If you do well, you don't get any credit; if you don't do well, the finger is pointed at you. That's what happened to Lynn, and a couple of months after that Gloucester defeat he decided to walk away and leave on his own terms.

I think he did a great job considering it was his first time as a head coach and when you see what he's done since it just shows how good he was. I think he's still a little bitter about what happened in Cardiff and I can't really blame him.

When I look back to that time, my main feeling about our lack of success is one of frustration and I know a lot of the senior players from the time feel the same. Given our playing resources, you can see why people have a go at Cardiff for underachieving. Although we won the league, the truth is we didn't come close to achieving our full potential.

By 2002, that star-studded team had started to be dismantled, with the likes of Rob Howley, Jonathan Humphreys, Neil Jenkins and Gareth Thomas all moving on. Personally, I think the people in charge at Cardiff let Rob and Humphs go too early. It seems that as soon as someone hits thirty in Wales, everyone thinks they are finished. But when you look at the likes of Humphs, Rob and people like Gareth Llewellyn, Colin Charvis and Mefin Davies, they've all played better since hitting the thirty mark. I think it's something we can all learn from.

We write people off way too early – and I'm not just saying that because I'm a thirty-something myself now! It's something I've always felt strongly about.

I'm not saying youth shouldn't be given its chance, far from it. I was given a break at a young age myself and I've always been a firm believer in the adage that if you're good enough, you're old enough. But, at the other end of the spectrum, I also think that if you're good enough, you're young enough. Just look at the players England had at their disposal when they won the World Cup in 2003, half those guys were in their thirties.

I just feel we're too quick to put people out to grass in this country. We tend to look at New Zealand and say, 'They do it there, so it must be right.' But New Zealand have got so many players: the bottom line is, they can afford to do it.

Cardiff made a big mistake when they let Rob and Humphs go. I think they just thought they'd let them go and chuck the youngsters in there, but it's not easy replacing players of that quality, especially when they still had some good years left in them – as they were to prove. Rob went on to win the Heineken Cup with Wasps, scoring the winning try in the final, and Humphs became a hero down at Bath, being made captain and playing a big role in reviving their fortunes, not to mention being recalled to skipper Wales in 2003.

Those two both left for England at the end of the 2001–02 season and they were followed out of the door by our South African coach Rudy Joubert, who returned home after only one year in charge.

That saw Dai Young taking over the coaching reins, which meant the club needed a new captain and that was to be start of another chapter for yours truly.

It was the dawning of a new era at the Arms Park, with changes at the helm, different expectations and the birth of the Blues just around the corner.

There were to be plenty of teething problems following that birth, as we struggled to make our mark in the new regional era, but I like to think over the last year or so that we've re-emerged as a real force again.

A lot of the credit for that has to go to Dai Young, who has put in a huge amount of work over the five years he's been in charge. Towards the end of his playing career you could always tell he'd be a really good coach. You can tell that straight away with some players and it was clear to me that Dai was going to make that transformation.

Not that it can have been easy for him. He was thrown into it with such a young side at Cardiff and the most experienced coach in the world would have struggled to achieve success in those circumstances. He had so much unfair stick, because if you look at the squad it had nowhere near the quality needed to get results. But that squad has been strengthened over the last couple of years and Dai has shown what he can do when he has the playing resources at his disposal.

I have to say he's been brilliant for me during my career. He's someone you can always go to for advice and he really knows what he's talking about, because he's been there through the tough times with Wales himself. Mind you, if he's got something on you or if he wants to take the mickey out of you, then you've had it, because he's got a really dry sense of humour.

In hindsight, life at Cardiff was never going to be like it was at Ponty. It's a much bigger club and it's got a lot more tradition. In Ponty, the focus was firmly on the rugby club. That's not the case with Cardiff. It's such a cosmopolitan city and rugby forms just one part of the fabric of the city.

So it's been a different experience these past nine years, but one I've thoroughly enjoyed. Everyone at the club has been really good to me and made me feel so welcome from the moment I arrived. The supporters have been great and so have the likes of Bob Norster and Peter Thomas, the chief executive and chairman respectively.

All in all then, it's a period in my career I look back on

with great fondness, albeit with a touch of frustration over what might have been.

# the three musketeers

I've been lucky enough to have met some amazing people through rugby, but there's been no one quite like Alfie.

That, of course, is the nickname by which Gareth Thomas, captain of Wales and the British Lions, is known throughout the game. He's been one of the biggest characters in Welsh rugby for more than a decade, but he's also been one of the most misunderstood and misrepresented. I like to think I know him as well as anyone in the game and the man I know is very different to the one that's often portrayed.

I first became friendly with Alfie when I broke into the Welsh squad in 1996, when I was with Pontypridd and he was playing for Bridgend. He'd picked up his nickname because of his supposed likeness to a big-snouted alien called Alf from a children's TV programme of the time and it's what everyone calls him to this day.

We clicked straight away and enjoyed each other's

company on and off the field. We also had a mutual friend in Leigh Davies, the Neath centre.

I've always been really close to Leigh, or 'Leigh Boy' as most people in the game know him. We played for Welsh Schools together, we were capped together at youth level and then I played for Wales with him as well. We both liked socialising and it's amazing now to think what we used to get up to. When we first got into the Welsh squad, we still used to go out drinking on weeknights. A lot of our friends were in college, so we'd meet up and go out with them on a Tuesday or a Wednesday night, which is unbelievable now when you look back on it.

But, in those early days of professionalism, that was just the way it was. And, in Alfie, we found a man after our own hearts. We both really hit it off with him and, by the end of 1997, Leigh and Alfie were team-mates at the Arms Park.

So by the time I signed for Cardiff in the summer of 1999, the three of us were really close and, for the next couple of years, we were pretty much inseparable. We were like the three musketeers, all for one and one for all. They were interesting times to say the least.

It's fair to say we all enjoyed a drink and off the field, we probably lived life a little bit fully. It was similar to what had gone on at Ponty, except with a smaller gang of us.

At Cardiff at the time, you had the older guys like Dai Young and Rob Howley who were married with families and they would look to spend time with them.

But myself, Alfie and Leigh Boy liked to go out. After every Cardiff game, especially the home ones, we would always be out in the city that night. There was the odd session on a Sunday as well.

I don't know if we held each other back, but when I look back at the way we conducted ourselves off the field we could have probably done a little bit more on the rugby front during that time, but we were enjoying ourselves and, at the end of the day, we were still young. We were only twenty-four, twenty-five, and the game was different then. It may have turned professional but, to a certain extent, in name only. A lot of people still had the same habits off the field as in the old amateur days. As a group, we hadn't really sussed out professionalism. We just thought it meant getting paid for playing.

When I think back to the times the three of us had together, what's funny is that people saw Leigh and Alfie as party animals, but not me. I always got away with it somehow. I don't know how. Perhaps it's because I'm a little bit quieter than the two of them and not as wild. But although I did my fair share of partying, I've never been tarnished with that reputation.

People would see that as the reason why the other two weren't getting selected or weren't playing as well as they could, whereas I never really had that accusation thrown at me. I just seemed to sneak under the radar. It's quite strange.

Those days seem an awfully long time ago now and it just shows how much things have changed when you think that players can hardly go out for a drink at all now without someone kicking up a huge fuss about it. We saw that last year when we went out in Edinburgh after playing Scotland and it ended up making headline news.

But that was the first time most of the boys had been out for weeks.

If there was a drinking culture in Welsh rugby during the early years of my career, there certainly isn't one now. The game has become professional in the fullest sense of the word. And, of course, it's been well documented how much Alfie has changed since those partying days and, apart from his immediate family, I've seen that change in him as much as anyone. I won my first cap with him, I was with him at Cardiff, I've been with him right the way through with Wales and now we are back together at the Blues.

It's really weird. He has changed and he hasn't, because he's still 'clean-off' for want of a better phrase. He's still bags of fun and has loads of energy and loves enjoying himself, but over the last few years he's probably realised how much the game means to him, whereas before he would kind of deny it and say it's just a sport. He really does care about it and he's grown into a senior player. He's someone who would readily admit that whereas he hated to have responsibility before, now he just thrives on it.

I think people misunderstand what kind of person he is. They will have watched him on that infamous *Scrum V* television programme the week after Mike Ruddock resigned as Wales coach in 2006 and they'll probably have come to the wrong conclusion about him from that.

The truth is he's a really passionate guy and when he cares about something he takes it to heart, and that was particularly the case when he was Wales captain, a job he was handed in the autumn of 2004. I've experienced that from when I was skipper at Cardiff. You take a lot home with you and you do take things to heart.

He was really passionate about the people he represented when he was Wales skipper and that passion rubbed off on the players around him. People who know him will say he's the kind of guy you want to go to war with. His fellow players think so much of him and have got the utmost respect for the bloke.

But I think the impression a lot of the public have of him is very different to the person I know. People seem to be really split in their views on him. Some people love him and some people hate him. You can see how he could polarise people: he's different.

He's straight down the line, but he's also a bit off the wall sometimes with the things he says and does and perhaps it rubs a lot of traditionalists up the wrong way. But he's just being himself and if he sometimes says something that upsets people he doesn't really care. He just says what he thinks. And when you consider what he's done in the game, he has definitely been hard done by on a number of occasions.

I would go as far as to say that he's achieved as much as any Welsh rugby player. I'm obviously biased, and I know it's a bold statement, but I honestly believe he's been Wales' greatest-ever rugby player.

Just look at his record. He can play anywhere from eleven to fifteen at international level and how many players can do that? He's Wales' record cap-holder, he's captained his country to a Grand Slam, he's captained the Lions and gone to the best team in Europe in Toulouse and won the Heineken Cup.

And yet you ask people in the street what Gareth Thomas means to them and a lot of them will only remember that *Scrum V* interview and Ruddockgate and that's really sad. But that's the way it is now. That's the way of the world with today's media.

People need to understand he was just trying to stick up for the boys in that TV interview because we had taken so much flak after Ruddock quit, with people accusing us of all kinds of things.

That's what Alfie is all about. He always puts the boys first, even if it meant putting himself in the firing line. He took all the flak for the squad after Ruddock's departure, which is why the boys look up to him like they do. He came in for a lot of stick at the time and was vilified in some quarters, something which I think was totally unfair. I know it affected him, because of all the stress and things, but you can't keep someone like Alfie down for long. He'll always come bouncing back.

I just hope people can push that *Scrum V* episode to one side and instead remember him for all the stuff he's done on the field. All I'll say is that I've played with and against a lot of the greats, and Alfie is definitely right up there with all of them.

I really believe our mutual mate Leigh Boy could have been in that category as well if he'd fulfilled his potential. Leigh was just an awesome player, one of the most naturally talented people I've ever seen in the game.

When he went out to Australia with the Welsh Schools side in 1994 he was phenomenal. For someone of his age, he was just so strong and so quick as well. He came back from that tour and then went straight into the Neath side

... and it was a really good Neath team at the time. It wasn't long before he was called up to the full Wales team and he had a fantastic start to his international career.

I can still remember him making his Five Nations debut against England at Twickenham in 1996, when he was still only nineteen, and giving Will Carling a really tough time in the centre. At that point, it looked as though he was going to be in the Wales team for years and years, but it never quite worked out like that.

Leigh will probably admit he should have done a lot more with all of his talent. But he probably wouldn't change a lot of what he did. He enjoyed life off the field as much as he did on it. He trained hard and played hard. That was his way and it's hard once you fall out of favour to fight your way back. But he's happy and that's the most important thing. What's also important is that the three of us remain really close friends to this day.

When I think back to those times we had together at Cardiff, I've got to mention Dan Baugh as well. He was definitely an honourable member of our little group and he also remains a good pal.

When I signed for Cardiff, I knew they had this crazy Canadian guy playing at No. 7 and I was thinking: 'What's training going to be like with this bloke?' I was expecting him to be scrapping with me straight away. But I couldn't have been more wrong.

From day one, he was just brilliant in making me feel really welcome. I was the valley boy who had come down to the big city and he went out of his way to make sure I fitted in. He was a big influence on me when I went down there. As it turned out, we ended up playing together at seven and six for a couple of seasons and those were some good times.

Dan was a real cult hero down at the Arms Park and, on his day, he was phenomenal. I've seen him win games virtually single-handedly and for a flanker to dominate a match like that he had to be special. Two of his performances that really stick out in my mind were against Saracens in the Heineken Cup at Vicarage Road in 2000 and down at Llanelli in a Welsh Cup game when he ran through half their team for a try.

He was brilliant in looking after me on the pitch and he is one of those who would run through a barn door for you. You couldn't really talk too much about gameplans or structures to Dan. You just had to let him get on with it. He was just flat out in every game, smashing people in the tackle and carrying the ball like his life depended on it. I used to be so grateful I was on the same side as him, because it's also fair to say he had a bit of a short fuse.

Off the field he was the perfect gentleman, but on it he was one of the scariest people you'll ever see. And when the switch went on, you just used to stay out of his way. You could tell when he'd gone. You'd try to calm him down, but his eyes would just be looking straight through you.

Sometimes when the switch went on he would go a bit over the top. I remember one particular cup game the club played at Pontypool, when the great scrum-half Dai Bishop was coming towards the end of his career. Dan had heard all about The Bish's reputation as a hard man and he just couldn't wait to get to grips with him. But he was on the bench that day, which meant he had to wait his turn. So by the time he finally came on as a sub, he was wound up like a top. And within about a minute of coming on, he'd dived over a ruck and butted The Bish. You thought 'here we go' and waited for the explosion. But The Bish just laughed at him!

Dan was the kind of player opposing fans used to love to hate because he played on the edge and was so physical in his approach to the game and so aggressive. But he was brilliant to play with and an absolute legend down in Cardiff. In some ways he was a bit like Dale McIntosh, my old Ponty back-row pal. The way they played, you could see why they picked up the injuries they did, because they put their bodies through so much. In the end, when his knees couldn't take it any more, Dan had to give in to injury, but what a player he was.

There were plenty of characters at the Arms Park during my early years at the club, including a few real 'old-school' types. One of those was Mike Rayer, the former Wales fullback. Mikey was Mr Cardiff. He was one of the few players at the club who was actually from the city and he was a real crowd favourite. He was in his second spell at the club at the time, having returned from a stint at Bedford, and he was coming towards the end of his career.

Having been through the amateur days, Mikey was definitely one of the old brigade, but he was really good fun. He didn't always see eye to eye with some of the new innovations that had come in with professionalism, like pool recovery sessions. He didn't enjoy those much and thought they were a bit over the top, so he would do his best to avoid them if he could.

I remember one incident in particular when we were up

in Scotland for a game against Glasgow. We were staying up there overnight afterwards, so, having won the match, we had a big night out and there were a few sore heads about the following morning.

We were due to have a pool recovery session first thing, but Mikey had other ideas. So he rang up Huw Wiltshire, our fitness coach – who was a huge influence on me in my younger days – put on a Scottish accent, pretending he was the manager of the hotel and saying we couldn't have the session because there was too much chlorine in the pool. Huw bought it hook, line and sinker and the session was called off!

But even though he was old school, Mike was still able to deliver the goods on the field in the professional era and he was a key figure for us in my first season at the club in 1999–2000 when we won the Welsh-Scottish league.

He captained the team during the first half of that campaign when the internationals were away at the World Cup and his experience and his ability to play in a number of positions behind the scrum was invaluable as we went on to clinch the title.

Another member of the old school in that team was Owain Williams, a back-row forward who had been capped by Wales during the amateur era. Owain would smoke I don't know how many fags a day and drink like a fish, but he'd be as fit as any of the so-called modern day pros and was as good a player as well. He was awesome. He would play every week and I would just look at him in amazement and wonder how he used to do it. Mikey was exactly the same.

You speak to all the boys that started out in the amateur days and then tasted a bit of the professional game and they'll always say they enjoyed their rugby a lot more when the game was amateur. I sometimes wonder whether I'd have preferred to have played in that era myself.

Don't get me wrong, rugby has given me a good living and I feel very fortunate to be paid for playing the sport I love but, obviously, when it is your livelihood, there's a lot more pressure involved. So you can see why people who played in both eras would have preferred the amateur days, when rugby was what you looked forward to at the end of your working week rather than actually being the critical part your working week.

It still mattered a hell of a lot when you got out on the field, but there was probably a bigger emphasis on enjoyment and on the social side of the sport. In the amateur days, Cardiff used to go on end-of-season tours to places like Australia and the boys who went on those trips will say that the memories formed there were the best part of their career. We've missed out on those kinds of experiences, because you don't have club tours any more. You only go away with the national squad and those are very much business trips.

Jonathan Humphreys, the ex-Wales captain, was another Cardiff player who had a brief taste of the amateur times and he was also a bit old school in some ways, especially when it came to modern attitudes towards training.

During the week, when it came to smashing each other and contact training he would hate it, but then every

Saturday he would be the first one in there putting his body where it hurt. He was a shrewd bloke and he couldn't see much sense in the mindless bashing we used to do sometimes when you used to get enough of it on Saturday. I find I'm a lot like him in that respect.

The boys called him 'Dangerous Brian', because he's just the clumsiest man in the world. But some opposing fans had less affectionate names for him. He wasn't the most popular with them and took loads of stick from the terrace, with people dubbing him 'Offside Humphreys'.

He was one of those who, when you didn't know him and played against him, you used to hate, because he was such a nuisance. I know that from my Ponty days. But then, when you trained with him and played with him and got to know the guy, he was exactly the kind of player you wanted in your team. He'd put his body where nobody else would and he was as brave as a lion. A lot of people thought he was finished when he left Cardiff, but he went on to have two or three more great seasons at Bath and ended up captaining them. He became a real cult hero at The Rec because, just like the fans at the Arms Park, they appreciated how he put his body on the line for the cause and how he led from the front.

We had a really good mix of people during those early days at Cardiff. You had your senior players, your Humphs, Mikey, Owain, Rob Howley, Dai Young, Neil Jenkins and Andrew Lewis, then you had the middle group, like myself, Alfie, Leigh Boy, Dan and Craig Morgan, plus the younger ones, like Jamie Robinson, Rhys Williams and Ryan Powell. We all got on well together and it was a good time.

Life may be different in the professional era and rugby is a serious business now, but you can still make good friends in the game and I've been lucky enough to make some great ones along the way.

## chapter 7

# the reluctant captain

If anyone had told me at the start of my career that I would go on to captain Wales and be skipper at Cardiff for three years, I wouldn't have believed them.

I've never really seen myself as a natural leader. Looking at myself as a player, I am probably a better lieutenant than captain. I am really loyal, but I don't think I'm forceful enough as a person to be the skipper and it's not something I've ever strived to be. Nevertheless, I've ended up doing the job for both club, region and country and I've always tried to do it to the best of my ability.

It was Graham Henry who set the ball rolling for me when he was Wales coach.

I'll never forget the moment: we were flying out to tour Argentina in 1999 and we changed planes in Paris. He just pulled me to one side in Charles de Gaulle airport and told me I would be captain for the first game in Tucuman.

I couldn't believe it and I remember ringing my mother up straight away to tell her. I was just over the moon, but then reality kicked in when I thought about the team I was going to be leading.

I knew Dai Young, Gareth Llewellyn, Jonathan Humphreys and Mark Taylor were all going to be playing in the game. I was never the most confident of people anyway, but all I was thinking was, 'How am I going to captain these guys? What am I going to try and say to them?' The initial euphoria, therefore, was followed by an overriding sense of panic.

Back then we used to have a team meeting the night before a game where the captain would speak to the players. Just to add to the pressure, there was a behind-the-scenes documentary being made on that tour and they came into film that meeting.

I remember thinking, 'Great, you are going to be on TV now making a fool of yourself.' I honestly can't remember what I said, but it's on that documentary if anyone has got a tape of it.

For a twenty-four-year-old with no captaincy experience in senior rugby, it was a daunting time. But the players were great. Rob Howley and Neil Jenkins were there on tour as well and they just told me to be myself, relax and go and play. Lynn Howells, my old Ponty coach, was on the trip as well as Henry's assistant, which helped. But it was still pretty nerve-racking.

We won that game against Tucuman 69–44 and I was made skipper for the other midweek match on tour against Argentina A in Rosario, which is probably best remembered for a stand collapsing, thankfully without anyone being seriously hurt, although I remember it more as being a really tough match which we lost 47–34, with a young Felipe Contepomi kicking twenty-four points for the hosts from fly-half.

The next time I captained Wales was against the USA in a pre-World Cup match at the Millennium Stadium later that year, when we won 53–24. For some reason they didn't cap that game, but I'm still taking it as my one and only win in an international, because I've lost all the others!

While it was a big honour to captain my country at such a young age, I didn't really feel cut out for the role. I am obviously a lot more comfortable in myself now and a lot more confident in my ability, but back then I was thinking I shouldn't even be in the same dressing room with some of the players who were in the Wales team that day – the likes of Allan Bateman, Gareth Llewellyn and Jonathan Humphreys – let alone captaining them. I felt I didn't belong there and I found it really difficult to try and impose my personality. I'm not that kind of person. I'm just not the imposing type, but that's what you need from a captain and that was even more the case back then. There was a lot of off-the-field stuff and a lot of talking and I wasn't comfortable with that. So it was never something I strived to be.

Yet, a couple of years later, I found myself as captain of the most famous club side in the world.

Dai Young had been skipper at the Arms Park for four years, but then, in the summer of 2002, he moved up to become head coach when Rudy Joubert returned to South Africa after a single season at the helm.

Following the departure of all the big names from the club, I was kind of the senior player there, so Dai asked me if I would take over as captain. I could see it was going to be a tough time, with Rob Howley having gone to Wasps, Jonathan Humphreys to Bath and Neil Jenkins back to Pontypridd, and Dai hanging up his boots as well. You take that kind of experience out of any side and you are going to struggle and we didn't really recruit well.

On top of that, there were some really tough acts to follow as skipper. If you look at the captain's board in the clubhouse, there are some absolute legends on it: people like Bleddyn Williams, Gerald Davies and John Scott.

But it's strange. I didn't have to think too hard when Dai asked me. I jumped at the chance, because I was comfortable in the environment at the club. I felt I'd earned both my stripes and the respect of the rest of the boys and I was more senior than pretty much all the boys there anyway. So it was a role I was comfortable to take on.

But I was under no illusions. I knew it was going to be a tough time. I remember sitting down with Dai and saying as much. To be fair, he knew it as well and both our fears were confirmed over the next couple of seasons.

It was difficult: we were a big club and we were struggling. You'd pick up the paper and people were saying how poor we were as a side, but it was still a great experience and I'm really glad I did it. I enjoyed the role and I think it brought the best out of me as a player. I always found I played better when I was captain. You do, because you want to prove something and you don't want things to go badly.

I eventually stood down as skipper in 2005 after three years in charge, during which time we were re-branded as the Cardiff Blues. My name is up there now on that captain's board and I'm proud of that. I was the first person to captain the new regional Blues team and no one can ever take that away from me.

Although we didn't do that well as a side, they must have thought something of me to keep me going as skipper. It would have been easy after such a bad first year to have said, 'He's obviously not producing the goods, let's get rid of him as captain,' but they stuck with me for three years and I'm very proud of that. It was a difficult time, but it probably helped me a hell of a lot, both as a player and a person.

It was during my first season in charge of Cardiff that I found myself leading Wales again, but this time it wasn't to be a midweek tour match or a non-cap game. I'd had a good start to the campaign, being named Welsh player of the 2002 autumn international series after the games against Fiji, Canada and New Zealand. But going into the 2003 Six Nations championship, captaining the side was the last thing on my mind.

Colin Charvis had been doing a good job at the helm and he was Steve Hansen's man. But then we lost our opening game out in Italy, which was a big shock to the system, and Colin was dropped. There was another big shock then when my old Arms Park pal Jonathan Humphreys was recalled four years after his last cap to lead the side for the England game in Cardiff, but then he got injured, so Wales were looking for their third skipper in as many matches. And that's when I was asked to take charge for the trip to Scotland.

I was over the moon to have been asked and grabbed

the opportunity with both hands. It was a no-pressure situation for me. I wasn't appointed on a permanent basis. It was a one-off thing and I was comfortable taking that on. Mind you, I was still pretty nervous just before the leading the side out at Murrayfield.

Not a lot was expected of us going up there after two defeats, but although we matched them for tries with a late rally, it wasn't quite enough to save us in the end. We were beaten 30–22, the same score as in Rome.

Humphs came back for the Ireland game at the Millennium, which we lost cruelly by a point to a late Ronan O'Gara drop goal, and was then sidelined again for the trip to France, which meant I was to be captain in Paris.

In the week before that game the Wales football manager Mark Hughes came along to speak to us and he gave a great talk. The Welsh soccer team were flying at the time and there was a lot of talk about football being the new national sport. But there was no crowing from Hughes. Instead he gave us a message that really sticks in my mind.

He said we were in exactly the same position his team had been a couple of years earlier, with people calling them the worst side in Welsh football history and with everyone slating them. But he said they knew at the time that they were doing the right things and weren't far off it and that they just needed the bounce of the ball to turn things around. He said it had worked for them and it could work for us. How right he was to be.

But there was to be plenty more pain before things were to turn our way, starting with that France game. We were well beaten in fairness, losing 33–5. It was a sad day, because defeat consigned us to the whitewash.

However, taking on the captaincy had made it a memorable Six Nations for me personally, and I had relished doing the job. It was a great bunch of boys to be in charge of and the support I had from everyone, particularly the senior players – like Gareth Thomas, Gareth Llewellyn, Mark Taylor and Colin Charvis – was superb.

But to finish bottom of the table without a win to our name came as a huge disappointment. And things weren't about to get any easier, with a tour to Australia and New Zealand coming up in the summer.

Our Kiwi coach, Steve Hansen, caused something of a stir by appointing four captains for that trip, myself, Colin, Stephen Jones and Robin McBryde. It was a bit strange, but it was just indicative of where we were at the time. We didn't have a standout candidate.

Colin obviously had the experience, but he wasn't the most popular person in Wales at the time after the Italy defeat, which he'd taken a lot of stick over. So Steve picked the four of us and said he would announce the Test captain when we got out there. I was fine with that. As it turned out, he asked me to do the job, which was a big honour.

We did really well in the first game when we took on the Wallabies in Sydney. No one expected us to do anything against them, but we gave a really good account of ourselves, with Jamie Robinson crossing for a great try after the break to put us right back in touch before we eventually went down 30–10. I was delighted with the effort from the boys and was proud of the team that day, even though we had lost.

We were so positive after that game; Australia had a really good side at the time and went on to reach the World Cup final later that year. So, even though we'd been beaten, we were delighted with the way we had played.

But then we came up against New Zealand in Hamilton and had a huge wake-up call. It was a real eye-opener and it left its mark on me in more ways than one.

The All Blacks were on fire that day and totally blew us away. They were so efficient in everything they did and we didn't have an answer to it. The way they came out after half-time was incredible. They were miles ahead of us and we ended up losing 55–3, with a certain Dan Carter scoring twenty points on his debut in the centre. Mark Taylor is one of most solid defenders you'd ever play with, but he had a really tough time with Carter that day and you knew then this kid was something special.

New Zealand were just far too good for us. It was a horrible experience and a pretty bruising one as well. Colin Charvis was knocked out in a huge hit from Jerry Collins, which was very worrying at the time, and I picked up a nasty gash under my eye, which forced me off for stitches. Steve Hansen admitted afterwards that it had been 'men against boys' and we all realised then just how much work we had to do.

We felt mentally shattered coming back from that trip. It had been a really tough tour following on from what had been a gruelling season, but it wasn't long before we were back together again for a series of four World Cup warm-up matches. First up was Ireland away; then three home games against England, Romania and Scotland.

At the time, Steve was trying to suss out who would be his captain for the World Cup in Australia a couple of months later. Gareth Thomas did the job out in Ireland; then Stephen Jones was in charge against England, when we lost 43–9 at the Millennium. I've been through some tough times with Wales, but my mood after that game was the lowest of the low. We'd lost by a record score at home to England and it was basically their B side.

It was at that point Steve Hansen pulled me in and said I was going to be captain for the World Cup. My immediate reaction was to feel really chuffed. But, after giving it serious consideration, I ended up turning him down.

I've been asked loads of time since then why I said no to the job, but the truth is it wasn't just one thing. It was a culmination of things.

At the time, I wouldn't say I had a frosty relationship with him, but I couldn't see where he was coming from. Being single-minded and a bit stubborn, you think you know it all really. I guess I was stuck in the old kind of ways.

So, at that time, he wasn't the favourite coach I'd ever worked with, let's put it that way. When things don't go well, it's easy to look for someone to blame and, back then, Steve was an easy target because he was getting a lot of flak from various quarters.

I remember him sitting me down and going through the points he wanted to get out of me as skipper and saying I needed to be strong and to pull the boys with me. I know he was just trying to help me and tell me what I needed to do. But that night I sat down and spoke to Sam and to my mother and I just said I didn't think I could do it. I didn't think I was the right man for it.

There were family factors to consider as well. We'd just had our first child, Mia, and I was finding it difficult because I was away for long periods of time. It was hard for Sam, even though family and friends were brilliant at helping out. The added pressure of me being captain at a really tough time wasn't what I needed.

When I came back from New Zealand, after we'd lost heavily out there, I was as down as I'd ever been in my rugby life. I was pretty unhappy for a while. I just thought that it shouldn't be happening. I think it affected my family a lot and I didn't want them to go through that again. I was finding it hard combining the responsibilities of being Wales captain and a young dad.

I can see why people might have been a bit confused by the decision at the time, because I was going to be away from my family for six weeks anyway at the World Cup, so what difference did it make whether I was skipper or not? But the way I looked at it at the time, it was the whole package. It's hard when you've got a family and you are away and I just felt to have the burden of being captain on top of that would have been too much and that it would have affected me.

So it was a culmination of family reasons and not being confident enough in myself. If you haven't got confidence in yourself then the boys will see through that and you are not the right person to do it. I just didn't think I was the right man at that time for the squad. Captaining your country is a much bigger deal than captaining your club or region. You're so much more in the spotlight and the eyes of the nation are on you. It's a massive responsibility.

There was a bit of a hoo-hah at the time over someone turning down the chance to be Wales captain, but it was the right decision to make. Having made it, I felt like a weight had been lifted from my shoulders and I was much happier.

People often ask me whether I regret that decision. Well I certainly regretted it when I got dropped for the World Cup quarter-final against England!

Ironically, it was the man who'd been handed the captaincy after I said no, Colin Charvis, who wore No. 7 instead of me in that game, with Jonathan Thomas keeping his place in the back row having done so well in the previous match against New Zealand, which I had been rested for.

I remember a lot of people saying that turning down the captaincy would prove the beginning of the end for me with Wales. I thought they might be right initially when I got left out for that England game and then found it hard to get back in the side.

But, as it turned out, the next three years went really well, both for me personally and for Wales, with Gareth Thomas taking over as captain and showing himself to be the right man for the job. So, eventually, it all worked out for the best.

But I still do have little regrets now and think to myself what could have been.

I never really sought the accolade of being skipper, but sometimes I think to myself it's such a big honour that perhaps I should have taken it. So, yes, I do regret it now.

chapter 8

# the great redeemer

**B**y the summer of 1998, Welsh rugby was at its lowest
ever point. We'd finished that year's Five Nations
with a 51–0 defeat to France at our temporary home of
Wembley. It was a result that marked the end of the road
for Kevin Bowring as coach.

Then we embarked on a tortuous tour of South Africa,
which is a hard enough place to visit when you've got a
full compliment of players, but virtually impossible when,
for one reason or another, you are missing as many key
men as we were for that trip.

In all, there were ten uncapped players in the tour
party, with my Pontypridd coaches Dennis John and
Lynn Howells being drafted in to run the show on a
caretaker basis.

The trip didn't begin too badly, with a stop-off in
Zimbabwe bringing a comfortable 49–11 victory in a game
that saw me win my sixth cap. But as soon as we arrived in
South Africa, things quickly started to go downhill.

We lost all four games ahead of the Test match and lost yet more players to injuries along the way, including yours truly. I ruptured a finger tendon in the defeat to Natal a week before the Test and that was the end of my involvement in the tour.

I was gutted because I really wanted to play against the Springboks. But I'll always remember the night before the match talking to Rob Howley, who was the tour captain. He'd got injured in the Natal match too, so he was out of the Test as well, and I just recall him turning to me that night and saying, 'This might be a good one to miss, you know.'

As it turned out, he was spot on, with Wales suffering a record 96–13 loss at Pretoria's Loftus Versfeld, conceding fifteen tries in the process. It was the highest ever score posted against a major international side and, but for a spilt ball in the last minute, the Boks would have brought up the century.

Their coach Nick Mallett rubbed salt in the wounds afterwards by describing us as 'probably the worst team in the world' and labelling the match as a 'pretty pathetic work-out' for the forthcoming Tri-Nations series against New Zealand and Australia.

Unfortunately, you couldn't really argue with him. As a nation, when it came to rugby, we were at the lowest point we'd ever been. It was going to take something or someone very special to turn things round. Enter Graham Henry.

After we came back from South Africa, his name started to be bandied about as a possible new Wales coach, with the WRU caught up in a tug-of-war with the

New Zealand Rugby Union for his services. In the end, the WRU got their man, with Henry signing a deal reported to be worth over £1 million.

The first thing I saw of him was probably the same as everyone else, when he was shown speaking at a press conference in New Zealand and came out with that famous quote: 'I'm going to coach Wales – and I'm leaving tonight.'

We had obviously heard of him from Auckland and what a good a job he had done there. He was clearly very highly respected and his record spoke for itself, having coached the Auckland Blues to two Super 12 titles in 1996 and 1997. But he was the first overseas coach we'd had in this country and, as a group of players, we just didn't know what to expect.

Yet from the moment he arrived, I liked him, even if he wasn't quite sure who I was! When he first came over, he obviously knew hardly any of the players, especially someone like me, and he'd tend to forget your name. He knew the likes of Scott Gibbs and Neil Jenkins, but he'd struggle with us younger guys and someone would have to prompt him.

Nevertheless, I must have made some kind of impression on him in his first couple of months here, because he selected me to play in his opening game in charge against South Africa in November 1998. It was awesome to be picked and it was the biggest game of my career up to that point.

The fact that the match was being played at Wembley made it stand out all the more. As a big Liverpool fan, I'd watched loads of games there on TV over the years, but never in my wildest dreams imagined playing there myself. The thought of running out at the Twin Towers was just amazing.

I can still clearly remember Graham's team talk before that South Africa game. It went along the lines of: 'These bastards have been bullying teams for the last 100 years and it's not going to happen today.' It really sticks in my mind as his first talk.

That South Africa side had a huge reputation and nobody gave us a chance, especially after what had happened in Pretoria just five months earlier. They had people like Gary Teichmann, Joost van der Westhuizen, Percy Montgomery and Mark Andrews in their team and they were on a record-breaking winning run at the time.

But the truth is we should have won that game. And if it hadn't been for the intervention of a long-haired loony, we might well have done. Midway through the second-half, we were on top and winning 20–17 thanks to an early Gareth Thomas try and Neil Jenkins' boot. We had done really well. But then on came this long-haired streaker from the crowd.

When play finally resumed after a lengthy delay, we seemed to have lost our momentum and spent the rest of the game on the back foot. We might still have held out for at least a draw but, as the game went into injury time, their flanker Andre Venter scored down in the corner and it was all over.

We were really disappointed in the dressing room afterwards, but we could take heart out of the fact that we'd put some pride back in the Welsh jersey. It was a really good game and I felt pretty pleased with the way things had gone for me in the back row alongside Colin Charvis and Scott Quinnell, both of whom had massive games.

We received huge praise as a team after that match, because we'd played really well and done so much better than anyone had expected. The press started calling us 'Henry's Heroes'. And that was after just one game – which we'd lost! But that just showed how desperate people had become for any kind of good news.

The following week we played Argentina down in Stradey and recorded our first win under Graham. They pushed us around in the scrum, but we played some excellent rugby that day and I was lucky enough to have a hand in a couple of our tries, while Charvy had another big game on the blind-side, touching down twice.

So all was rosy in the garden. People were going on about the re-emergence of Welsh rugby and everyone was talking about Henry. The WRU had dubbed him 'The Great Redeemer' in adverts for that autumn's game, which didn't go down too well with some church figures, who claimed it was blasphemous, but the name really stuck. It seemed pretty appropriate given the way he'd turned round our fortunes in such a short space of time.

We had our own name for him by then – 'Scrunchie'. That was because of the way he used to scrunch his face up. I can't remember who came up with that first, but that was to be our name for him for the next four years.

What Graham did for us straight away was make us very organised as a team. He was just so comprehensive in his analysis of the opposition and the way he wanted us to play. When you went out on the field, you didn't have any doubts about the gameplan or what your job was. His planning and preparation were spot on. The guy was just amazingly thorough.

In terms of tactics, one of the first changes he made was to bring in the now-famous 'pod' system. In simple terms, that basically involved splitting the pack into two. So, for example, after a line-out the non-lifting group would go to the next contact and then the lifters would go to the second contact, whereas before everyone would just follow the ball. That was a big difference for the boys, but we got used to it pretty quickly.

There were changes off the field as well. Our first Five Nations match that season was against Scotland up in Murrayfield. We turned up at the hotel in Edinburgh on the Thursday night and the fridge in the team room was full of beer. That hit us for six.

Graham's idea was that he wanted all the boys to have a drink together, not to have a session but to relax and have one or two beers. His attitude was: 'You are all adults and you all know what works for you.' The senior players really bought into it and enjoyed what Graham was doing. I know from speaking to Steve Hansen that they did that with the New Zealand team as well. They were trying to get them away from binge drinking. Their thinking is that if there's beer available and the players have one or two then they won't go on a binge.

Given how well things had gone during the autumn, we went into that 1999 Five Nations campaign with high hopes and with a great deal of public expectation. Thousands of supporters travelled up to Edinburgh for the opening game and Graham was clearly taken aback by it all. He couldn't believe the number of Welsh fans camped outside the team hotel.

Those fans were to end up going home disappointed, as we lost 33–20 after leading at half-time. I kept my place for the next match against Ireland at Wembley, but after we lost that one as well – going down 29–23 to an Irish team inspired by Keith Wood and David Humphreys – I found myself left out of the side for the trip to Paris.

I was replaced by a New Zealander called Brett Sinkinson, who qualified for Wales through his grandfather, or so I and everyone else thought at the time ... but more of that later.

I felt pretty hard done by when I got dropped because I thought I had been playing quite well. I certainly thought I had done well in the autumn and felt as though I had gone okay in the first two championship games, but Graham obviously decided, following two successive defeats, it was time for a change. You always feel you are an easy target as a youngster, because they are not going to drop any of the senior players.

But the way Brett played when he came in, I couldn't have had any complaints at all. He had an outstanding debut against France in a 34–33 victory that was to mark the start of a ten-match winning run, which included famous victories over England and South Africa.

Those ten games marked a frustrating time for me, because as glad as you are that the boys are doing well, you still think that's the end of your international career. Brett had been a revelation and there was no doubt, given the form he was in, that he deserved to be playing instead of me. Even though I was only twenty-three, I was starting to think I was never going to get back into the team. That's how you do think. The guy was just playing so well.

But, in fairness to Graham, he still picked me to go on the summer tour to Argentina and gave me the chance to captain the midweek side. It came as a big boost to my confidence.

We won both Tests out there, a real achievement, and then we came home to face the Springboks in the first ever game at the new Millennium Stadium.

I was a water boy for that match, carrying on the drinks for the players during any breaks in play. That job had been given to myself, Gareth Llewellyn, Geraint Lewis and Neil Boobyer. You might imagine that would have been quite a demoralising role, being so close to the action without being able to get involved, but the amazing thing was you were chuffed to be called in as a water boy for that match because you then knew you were going to be in the World Cup squad. That was to be our last game ahead of the squad being picked. So it was the one and only time you wanted to be a water boy!

It was a really surreal occasion. The stadium still wasn't completed and it resembled a building site, with workmen in hard hats watching from one end of the ground. The place was less than half-full with only about 27,000 people in there, but the atmosphere was electric nevertheless and it proved an historic day as we recorded our first ever victory over South Africa – almost exactly a year after we'd been humiliated in Pretoria.

At that point Henry could do no wrong. He was a national hero and probably the best-known man in the country. His predecessor, Kevin Bowring, had had quite a low profile, but Graham was totally different. He was a natural in front of the cameras and came across really well. He wasn't short on opinions either and didn't mind sharing them with people. I can remember watching him on Welsh TV and they would be asking him questions about farming and things. But that's the profile he had and how highly thought of he was at the time. The guy was walking on water.

He was great at dealing with the media and he knew how to turn on the charm in public. But there was also a real edge to the guy. He didn't lose his temper that often, but when he did, you certainly knew about it. In the first Test against Argentina in Buenos Aires, we were losing 23–10 at half-time. I wasn't involved in the match, but I was in the changing room at the break and Graham gave the boys a real roasting. He was kicking the water bottles and everything. At that point I was quite glad not to have been playing!

You learn a lot about people behind the closed doors of a dressing room. What you tend to learn, above all else, is that everyone's human.

In his first game in charge against South Africa at Wembley, it was 14–14 at half-time and we were bouncing off the walls when we came in because we were doing so much better than anyone had anticipated. But Graham gave this really measured team-talk, saying all the right things, before leaving us to get ready for the second half. Before going back out, I needed the loo so I went to the toilets, which were in a different area to the changing rooms at Wembley, and Graham was sitting in there having a fag. Obviously the nerves were getting to him as well.

I always liked him as a person. He had a good sense of humour, he was quite dry and I got on with him pretty well. But he could be intimidating, especially for a youngster. He had such an aura around him and, as a young player, he's not somebody you felt comfortable having a conversation with. It was a little bit like a teacher-pupil relationship and you didn't want to get on the wrong side of him.

But, looking back, he was brilliant with me. He must have thought something of me to give me the captaincy for those midweek games in Argentina and he put me in charge again for the uncapped pre-World Cup match against the USA.

That was one of three warm-up games we had at the new stadium in August 1999, along with full Tests against France and Canada, and we won all three to extend our winning run. There was a real buzz in the country at the time and a genuine feeling was starting to grow that we could go a long way in the World Cup, a tournament we would be hosting.

As part of our build-up, we went all around Wales on training camps, to places like Tenby, Brecon and Caernarfon, and we were treated like royalty wherever we went.

We were full of confidence going into the World Cup and we kept the momentum going by starting off with pool victories over Argentina and Japan at the now full-capacity Millennium.

I played at six against the Japanese because Colin

Charvis was suspended and it went well, so Graham kept me there for the next match against Samoa. But that was to be the end of our winning streak.

At the time, Scott Quinnell was immense for us at No. 8 and the Samoans just targeted him and took away our gameplan. That was a bit of a wake-up call for us, but we still made it through to the quarter-finals where we played Australia. And that's a game we should have won.

With Colin available for selection again I was in the stand for that one, but it was another Colin – Kiwi referee Colin Hawke – who grabbed the headlines because of a couple of controversial decisions.

The other thing that sticks out in my mind is the ovation the boys got from the Cardiff crowd after the game. They did a lap of honour and were really well received. Although we had lost, there was a general feeling that we were back as one of the top sides again.

So we went into 2000 and the new millennium with a real sense of belief and optimism. Wales had made a big success of staging the World Cup and the national team was now a force to be reckoned with once more, thanks to efforts of the Great Redeemer.

It seemed as though we had regained the respect of world rugby. But it wasn't long before we were to become the laughing stock once more.

# grannygate grief

There aren't many things I look back on in my career with frustration, but the Grannygate saga is definitely one.

That was the name given to the row which erupted in the spring of 2000 when it emerged that Wales had been fielding two ineligible players, New Zealanders Brett Sinkinson and Shane Howarth.

The whole episode was a disaster for Welsh rugby and did nothing for our image within the world game. But, for me, it had a much more personal connotation, because Sinkinson was the man who had been keeping me out of the Wales team for the previous year.

To understand the background to all this, you have to remember what Graham Henry's brief was when he was appointed national coach in the summer of 1998. He had been brought in to turn around Wales' flagging fortunes and, given his bumper salary, the WRU were after rapid results. So Henry was looking for a quick fix.

It didn't take him long to realise that we didn't have the strength in depth to be a top international side. So he decided to go down the same route Jack Charlton had done when he took over as manager of the Republic of Ireland soccer team.

Charlton had hunted out any players with Irish ancestry, drafting in the likes of Andy Townsend, Ray Houghton and John Aldridge, and the result was that Eire became a real force on the world stage. Henry set about doing the same thing for Wales and called up Sinkinson and Howarth, who were both eligible through their grandparents – or so we all believed at the time.

In fairness, both of them were instant hits in the team. Shane had already played for the All Blacks but, under the rules at the time, you were allowed to represent more than one country provided you were qualified for both. So he joined the Welsh cause and launched his second Test career in style, making an outstanding debut at full-back against South Africa in Henry's first game in charge at Wembley in November 1998.

He immediately established himself as a fixture in the side and, later on that season, he was joined by Neath flanker Sinkinson, who replaced me on the open-side for the Five Nations match in Paris.

I was obviously disappointed at the time, but I couldn't have any complaints given the way Brett played against the French and he kept up that form as Wales went on a ten-match winning run during 1999.

It was a difficult one: the pair of them obviously weren't Welsh and they hadn't had the same upbringing as us but, on the other hand, we were playing so well as a team. With my personality being the way it was, I kind of went along with it, just kept going and kept my head down. With the way Brett was performing, there was no way I could really feel hard done by. But all that was about to change.

It was March 2000 when the bombshell dropped. We'd made a disappointing start to the inaugural Six Nations, losing to France and England either side of beating new boys Italy, but that was soon overshadowed by the news that broke next.

I can just remember Graham coming into the team room and saying: 'We've got a bit of a problem boys.' It turned out there was a story in the press saying Shane and Brett weren't qualified to play for Wales after all.

We couldn't believe it. I don't think any of us had had any inkling that there was anything wrong. I certainly hadn't. I thought it was all kosher. There wasn't any reason to think otherwise. These boys came in, they were great players, they made a big difference to us and you didn't have any reason to think they weren't qualified. You just assumed that if the management had selected them, then their eligibility must have been fine.

But, according to the press reports, Brett's grandfather wasn't from Carmarthen, as we'd been led to believe, but Oldham, while there were doubts cast over Shane's qualification as well, and both of them were withdrawn from the squad for the upcoming game against Scotland.

From what I can remember, there was no question of anything sinister having gone on. We just saw it as one big cock-up and that not enough checks had been made. We were almost laughing about it at the time, thinking how could such a thing get through.

As time went on, and, as the years have gone by, I've become increasingly bitter about it. As a kid, your dream is to play for Wales and you work your socks off to get to that stage. To get there and then to have it taken away from you because mistakes were made over someone else's right to pull on the red jersey is hard to take.

Brett coming in probably cost me something like ten to fifteen caps and you can't help but wonder what might have been, especially when I think of some of the games I could have played in and some of the great victories I missed out on, like beating England at Wembley and South Africa at the Millennium Stadium.

I watched that April 1999 England game with all my mates at Cilfynydd Rugby Club, just outside Pontypridd, and I remember the place going wild when Scott Gibbs scored at the end and then Neil Jenkins put over that winning conversion. It was one of the greatest victories for years, because England were such a good side then and we had turned them over against all the odds.

I am sure if you talked to all the boys who played in that game they would say it was one of the highlights of their careers – and I wasn't part of it and I could have been. Given the circumstances, it's hard to look back on occasions like that. Of course, we might not have won if I'd played in those games, but I'd like to think I could have played my part.

So I am quite bitter about it and not just for myself, but for other open-sides who were around at the time, like Kingsley Jones, Jason Forster and Ian Boobyer. I've been lucky. I've had my chance since then. But some boys would have been at their peak back then and if I'd have had their chance of twelve to eighteen months of international rugby taken away from me because mistakes were made over who was eligible to have been playing for Wales, then I would have been upset.

The same goes for the full-backs around at the time. Who missed out while Shane was in the side? My mate Kevin Morgan was the main one to lose out there. He could have had fifteen or twenty more caps to his name and I am sure he feels exactly the same as me about what happened.

Brett and Shane were great players and I got on with both of them pretty well. It's just sad to think that true Welsh players lost out on that.

After the story broke, things went crazy for a while and everyone's eligibility was being scrutinised like mad. The daftest one happened to my Cardiff team-mate Nick Walne. He found himself caught up in the middle of it all when he was withdrawn from the Wales A team after his eligibility had been called into question.

Now that was just bonkers. I played with Nick for East Wales Under-11s, Wales Schools, Wales Youth, right the way through, so he was as Welsh as you get. He might have been born in Scunthorpe, but he moved to Wales at an early age and spent all his childhood in this country. Yet because he had moved away to England to study at Cambridge University and then joined Richmond, it was being suggested that he had broken his residency period and wasn't qualified for Wales any more. That was plain daft. You can't just stop being Welsh. Nick's eligibility was never in doubt as far as I was concerned and, thankfully, the powers-that-be saw sense in the end. But, as I said, it was a crazy time for a while.

Of course, Howarth and Sinkinson weren't the only overseas players Henry drafted in. There was also Jason Jones-Hughes, who became the subject of a tug-of-war between Wales and Australia; South African centre Andy Marinos; and Kiwi full-back Matt Cardey; while the English-born Peter Rogers had been playing out in South Africa.

All of those qualified legitimately through family connections, but Henry also had plans to bring over a group of young southern hemisphere players without any Welsh links at all with a view to them eventually qualifying through residency. That proved a step too far and he was forced to drop the plan after a public outcry, although one of the youngsters did still come over – a South African by the name of Hal Luscombe who, of course, has gone on to play a number of times for Wales.

You can't really knock Graham for what he did and I for one can totally understand why he did it. He was just doing his job in trying to get us back up to a level where we could compete and he was looking for any kind of edge for Wales. In fairness to him, it worked. He put us back on the map as a side and we had some great times as a result.

But it backfired badly with Grannygate. That whole affair didn't cast Welsh rugby in a good light at all and, for a couple of us who lost out personally, it left a very bitter taste in our mouths.

Obviously the regulations have been tightened up a lot since then, which is a good thing, but the whole eligibility issue is still a big point of contention. I have to admit, I'm somewhat torn on the subject.

I am really good mates with Dale McIntosh, the Kiwi No. 8 who I played with at Pontypridd and who was able to play for Wales after living here for a number of years. I know he was as proud as anyone to pull the Welsh jersey on and the same goes for another New Zealander, Sonny Parker, and the Aussie-born Brent Cockbain, who both also qualified through residency.

But having been in the situation where I was kept out of the side by someone who wasn't a Welshman, I can see why people are against players coming in from overseas and then playing for Wales. I've been as affected as anyone by it and, when your dream as a kid is to play for your country and that dream is being denied by someone who hasn't dreamed of that all his life, I can see how frustrating it is for people.

So, if I was drawing up the rules, part of me would say you can only play for a country if you have been born and bred there. But that would mean the likes of Brent and Sonny would never have been able to play for Wales and I wouldn't have wanted that. I've got a huge amount of time for those boys. I've seen how much effort they've put in and what they've brought to the table, both on and off the field. They are as committed as anyone and they've been a huge plus for Welsh rugby. You wouldn't want them out of the team, because you've played with them and you know they give everything as much as anyone else.

So it's a difficult one and a real double-edged sword. My personal experiences mean I can see both sides of the argument. On reflection, I think what I'd like to see happen is the length of the residency period increased from three years to five. That would mean you would have to be really committed to your 'adopted' country and it would deter any people who were just looking for a flag of convenience to play under.

The whole Grannygate period was a really turbulent time for Wales because we also lost our conditioning coach Steve Black midway through that 2000 Six Nations campaign.

A larger-than-life Geordie, Blackie had been brought in by Henry a couple of years earlier on the recommendation of the Samoan skipper Pat Lam, who had worked with Graham at Auckland and then with Blackie at Newcastle.

He wasn't your typical fitness coach, either in terms of his appearance – what with his portly physique – or his methods. But for eighteen months, it really worked.

Blackie played a huge part in making us believe as a side. He was brilliant for the boys because, psychologically, he gave them confidence. He used to tell you you were the greatest and the best player in the world and you would have bags of belief.

Off the field, he was superb for me. He was the guy I rang up when I didn't know whether or not I wanted to stay at Pontypridd or go to Cardiff. That was how highly I thought of him. He was a great guy and if you wanted to talk to him about anything he was brilliant. You speak to any of the boys; he was great for that side at that time.

He was from a football background originally and in football they treated players a little bit more like adults.

And that was how he treated us. The attitude with Graham and Blackie was: 'You know what works for you, you're old enough, you're men, we'll let you get on with it.' That was especially the case with the more senior players. You had people like Jenks, Rob Howley and Scott Gibbs at the top of their game and it worked for them.

So for the first year or so everything was fine, but then questions started to be raised about our fitness. The former Australian coach Bob Dwyer set the ball rolling in the lead-up to that 2000 Six Nations by saying we weren't fit enough and describing the Quinnell brothers – Scott and Craig – as fat. That was over the top, but I think some of the criticism was probably fair.

In 1998 and 1999 the boys were in really good nick and our performances proved that. We won ten in a row and more than held our own fitness-wise with the likes of England, South Africa, Australia and France. But perhaps in 2000 we weren't in condition. Our results show that.

When we went up against England at Twickenham that year, they were so much quicker, so much stronger and so much more powerful than us. I think that was a huge wake-up call about how far ahead they were of us. We had great players, boys who had been on the Lions tour, but the English had moved on so far beyond the field of play. They were just streets ahead of where we were at the time. The truth was we may have been mentally conditioned, but we certainly hadn't been physically conditioned.

Blackie got a lot of flak after that England game and I think it started to get to him. He had a heart of gold and his whole ethic was he just wanted to do what was best for the boys. Then people started to try and dig into his private life and his past. I remember him saying: 'I don't need this.' He wasn't here for that. He was really peeved.

He had two young boys who were getting caught up in it and getting stick at school and I think that was just the final straw for him. You couldn't blame Blackie for just going back up north. It had all got a bit unsavoury and people were looking for things that weren't really anything to do with rugby.

Looking back, perhaps I didn't develop physically as I could have done as a young player during that period, but mentally and emotionally Steve was brilliant and for those first couple of years under Henry he was what we needed to give us belief. I think the fact that Jonny Wilkinson speaks so highly of him says an awful lot.

Despite all the problems during that 2000 Six Nations campaign, we somehow managed to put them behind us and finish off with victories over Scotland and Ireland. Then, the following year, I was part of the Welsh team that recorded one of the best results of all under Henry when we won out in France. But that was to be the last great result of his reign.

That summer he took charge of the Lions in Australia and you could kind of tell he was a different person when he came back. He had taken so much flak over losing the series and the way the tour had been run, with players criticising him personally, and mentally it had taken its toll on him.

I wasn't involved in the autumn internationals in 2001 because I'd done my shoulder on the Lions tour, so I had to watch on as we lost at home to Ireland and Argentina.

It was the first time the Welsh public had really started to turn against Henry and the writing was on the wall.

Going into the 2002 Six Nations, a lot of the senior players who had underpinned his team, like Neil Jenkins, Scott Gibbs, Garin Jenkins and Dai Young, were missing either through injury or retirement. We had a lot of inexperienced players and we went out to Ireland for the opening game and got absolutely stuffed. We played really poorly that day and were just blown off the park.

Coming home from Dublin, I remember we were walking through the airport and some Welsh supporters started singing, 'We've got the worst team in the land.' That was my first experience of that kind of thing and it was a real low. You wouldn't have wished that trip home on your worst enemy.

That game was the last straw for Graham. I remember we met up for training a couple of days later and it was strange, you sensed something was in the air. We were then called in for a team meeting. Whispers had got round that Graham was going and he came in and just explained he was leaving. He said he'd really enjoyed his time in Wales, but felt he had taken the team as far as he could and wanted to get back home to New Zealand.

So how should history judge Graham Henry's time in charge of Wales? Well, despite the Grannygate debacle, I think he should be judged favourably.

Admittedly, there wasn't as much emphasis on development as there was to be under Steve Hansen and Scott Johnson, and I felt at the time that younger players like myself weren't getting that much attention. But Graham was looking for immediate success, so he emphasised the here and now and the organisation of the team, and in all fairness it worked. For the first two years it was brilliant and his record during that period speaks for itself.

Overall, he was a huge plus for Welsh rugby. We can be very insular in Wales in our thinking and in our ideas and I just think he opened everyone's minds up a lot. He's the most organised coach as regards to having a gameplan and analysing the opposition that I've ever worked under.

He was also instrumental in improving off-the-field facilities for the team. When he first came over he couldn't believe how poor they were. Back then, we used to train at the Pencoed Equestrian Centre in the muck down there. Graham was influential in getting the indoor arena built at the Vale of Glamorgan complex, on the outskirts of Cardiff, and that's become a huge asset to the squad.

So, even though I might have suffered along the way, I'd be the first to acknowledge that old Scrunchie was a definite positive for Welsh rugby.

## chapter 10

# flogging a dead lion

**W**hen I look back on my earliest memories of the British Lions, it's not Perth, Pretoria or Palmerstone North that springs to mind, but the Heath Hospital, Cardiff. That's where I spent a large chunk of the summer of 1989, at the age of fourteen, after undergoing a thyroid operation.

My stay there coincided with the Lions tour of Australia and watching that tour on television in hospital stands out as one of my biggest childhood rugby memories. I can remember Robert Jones and Nick Farr-Jones fighting in the second Test in Brisbane and Ieuan Evans scoring the try to win the series under David Campese's nose in the final Test in Sydney.

That was when I really started to take notice of the Lions. Up until then, they hadn't made that much of an impression on me. But that tour really stuck in my mind and from then on that was the dream – to become a Lion. That's what I wanted to do.

Eight years later I got my first taste of what it was like to be a Lion – or at least a Lion's chauffeur! It was 1997 and Ian McGeechan's side had just recorded a memorable series victory over the Springboks in South Africa. One of the big heroes of that trip was Neil Jenkins, my team-mate at Pontypridd, who I also worked with at Just Rentals, the club's main sponsors.

All his family had gone out to watch him play in South Africa, so he rang me up from out there and asked if I would pick him up from Heathrow. He knew I was off-season and thought I had nothing else to do. Anyway, I said yes, so I got up in the middle of the night, because they were landing first thing in the morning, and drove up there to pick him up.

I remember standing in the arrivals lounge where they all came through and they'd obviously been on the lash throughout the trip home. You should have seen the state of Jeremy Guscott and Rob Wainwright as they were coming through. Not that Jenks was much better. After I got him in the car, I had to stop about 100 yards down the road for him to throw up out of the window!

After that, I was just talking to him all the way home and asking him questions non-stop. That 1997 tour had been massive and had really captured people's imagination, not least mine. It was probably the first Lions trip that received such huge media coverage, with Sky TV showing all the games and hundreds of supporters going out there. I had watched it as a fan over here and I just wanted to know everything about it. So speaking to Neil on the way home was awesome.

Jenks was huge at that time. When we got home, we

drove through Llantwit Fardre and there were banners saying 'Welcome home Neil' draped across the streets. Seeing that, I just thought I would love to be part of a tour like that. So being selected for the 2001 Lions trip to Australia became a firm target in my mind.

But four years later, at the beginning of 2001, it really wasn't in my mind at all. I didn't think I had any chance of making it. I wasn't in the Wales team, with Colin Charvis having worn the No. 7 jersey throughout the autumn internationals, so I couldn't see there was any way of me fulfilling my Lions dream.

But then, a week or so before the opening Six Nations match against England, I got my first inkling that I might be in with a shout of starting, when Graham Henry talked about using me as a line-out target – and sure enough I was in, with Colin moving to the blind-side.

We had really high hopes going into that first game in Cardiff because we thought we had a good side. But England at that time were just way ahead of us – in fact they were streets ahead of everyone. Will Greenwood was awesome that day, scoring a hat-trick of tries, as we were beaten 44–15. The width they put on their game was superb and they did to us what we were to do to sides four years later when we won the Grand Slam.

We went up to Murrayfield next and drew 28–28 with the Scots, thanks in the main to Jenks' kicking, and then the Ireland match was called off because of the Foot and Mouth outbreak.

I felt I had played pretty well up in Scotland, but I still wasn't thinking about the Lions. For me, it was the French game that was the real turning point.

We beat them 43–35 out there and that's when I started thinking I could be in with a shout. There was a lot of talk about the Lions after that game and how many Welsh boys had put themselves forward for it and my name was mentioned a few times. Up until then, I never thought I would get picked. But to beat France in Paris was huge and while Rob Howley and Scott Quinnell rightly took most of the plaudits, I had done okay and there were murmurings that I could go.

On the day the squad was named, I was training with Cardiff at the indoor arena at UWIC in Cyncoed, so I didn't actually hear it being announced on the radio. But I didn't have to wait long to find out the news, because Dan Baugh came sprinting out of the physio room, picked me up and screamed, 'You're in!'

It wasn't a total shock because, since the Six Nations, people had printed their probable squads and I'd been mentioned in a few of them. But I still didn't really believe there was any way they were going to pick me, because there were a lot of good flankers about. England's Neil Back was obviously the main No. 7 at the time; then you had Budge Pountney of Scotland and David Wallace of Ireland; plus guys like Colin Charvis and Richard Hill who could play both six and seven. So there were loads of options in the back row and I thought I was never going to get selected.

After I found out I was in, the rest of that day was just a massive blur. Not that I thought it was going to be that great to start with. I remember ringing my mates up one by one and asking them whether they fancied going out in the evening for a drink to celebrate and they were saying:

'No it's all right, we've got things on.' I was really down. I kept thinking this is one of the biggest days of my life and no one wants to share it with me.

I went home and I was sitting in the house feeling sorry for myself, when all of a sudden everyone turned up. Without me knowing, all my family and friends had arranged a big party and it was just a great night. That day was probably the best feeling I'd ever had, because you'd achieved everything you could possibly achieve. It was the ultimate.

Of course, looking back it wasn't anything of the sort. The 'ultimate' would have been to have won a place in the Test team and that should have been my goal. But the truth was I was just glad to be there and was in awe of all these guys like Martin Johnson, Keith Wood, Lawrence Dallaglio and Jonny Wilkinson. I wasn't like Scott Quinnell or Dai Young who probably put themselves on the same level as those people.

That lack of confidence was a downfall of mine for a long time and probably held me back when I was younger. I was very naive then and it's probably the wrong way to be.

The coach for that Lions trip to Australia was Graham Henry and he had selected ten of his Welsh players, which led to people criticising him for picking too many, especially with England having topped the championship that season.

It must have been difficult for Graham. England had enjoyed enormous success playing a certain way and the shadow of their coach, Clive Woodward, was never far away during that tour. I don't know if the English guys felt Clive should have been there rather than Graham, or whether they had an issue with the fact Graham was a Kiwi. We were obviously used to him, but I'm not sure how the English boys felt.

The week before we left, we all met up at a really plush place called Tynley Hall in Hampshire. As soon as we met up as a group, the biggest thing I noticed was how far the English players were ahead of us off-the-field and in terms of their preparation. I was rooming with Phil Greening, the Wasps hooker, and I remember him pulling out this huge bag of vitamins and supplements. He explained how the English players had had their hair samples taken to Harley Street for testing and all these things they were doing. After training sessions they'd all be mixing their protein shakes up and taking their supplements. We just didn't do anything like that. The only herbal supplement us Welsh boys would have was a cup of tea.

Now you wouldn't get anyone more professional than Rob Howley, Dai Young or Jenks, but the advice the English boys were getting at the time was phenomenal. It was streets ahead of us. They had obviously spent loads of money on the backroom staff; I'm sure it came as a shock to the Irish and the Scottish guys, too.

The other thing that struck me immediately was how many different coaches there were. There were obviously nowhere near as many as we were to have in New Zealand in 2005, but at the time there seemed to be a hell of a lot of them and that was to end up counting against us over the next couple of months.

As soon as we arrived in Australia, the training was just crazy from day one – and I mean day one. We arrived in

Perth at about 12 o'clock at night and we were up at 7am the next morning for our first training session. Apparently that's supposed to help you get over your jetlag. That was the theory, anyway. I beg to differ on that one! Usually your first session after a long journey is maybe a game of touch rugby and just a loosener, but that morning was just flat out straight away and we were all thinking: 'What's going on here?' But it just kept on like that day after day.

The problem was we had so many coaches and they all wanted a piece of you.

You had Andy Robinson, the forwards coach, who demanded time with you; Graham was the attack coach and he'd want to do an attacking session; and then you'd always finish with Phil Larder, the defence coach. This would just be every day and the sessions would go on forever, with a lot of intensity, because everyone was trying to push their case.

The boys kept battering each other and our physio Mark 'Carcass' Davies was working twelve-hour days patching people up. He would be in his physio room from 7am until 10pm at night and he'd be nodding off on the bus on the way to training in the morning.

On the 1997 tour, he'd picked up the nickname of 'Gullivers' as in 'Gulliver's Tours', because the players were ribbing him that he was just out there on a jolly. But it was a very different story this time round. He hardly had time to draw breath.

It just seemed all we did was train and that's what really got to the boys. There was hardly anything going on off the field, it was just all rugby, rugby, rugby. Anyone who has been in that environment will tell you you've got to have time to switch off and do something else.

You'd see the books and videos of previous Lions tours and there'd be shots of players taking in the sights of whichever country they were in and meeting up with the locals. I particularly remember watching the behind-the-scenes DVD of the 1997 tour and seeing how much went on away from the rugby on that trip.

But in 2001 all we saw was the hotel and the training field. What made things worse was the fact the boys obviously knew there was so much to do in Australia. It's a great country with so much to see, but we didn't really see any of it.

We were in Townsville, up in Queensland, for one game and we didn't even have a chance to go to the Great Barrier Reef, because we were just training and playing. It was over-the-top preparation in my eyes.

I think the problem was that Graham was under a lot of pressure to deliver results. The success of the 1997 tour had put pressure on him to be really successful this time. The issue was, a lot of the boys had been on that '97 trip to South Africa and remembered what it had been like. Apparently that had been an old-school tour and, off-the-field, it had been awesome. For the survivors of that trip, this tour fell a long way short of their expectations.

You could sense the frustration brewing and it came to a head on the eve of the first Test in Brisbane when the English scrum-half Matt Dawson criticised the training regime in his newspaper column. You could totally understand where he was coming from, because this tour had come at the end of what had been such a tough season and here we were being flogged.

His comments created a hell of a stink and he ended up getting fined. Because we won that first Test he was made to look a bit foolish at the time, but he had probably only said publicly what a lot of people were thinking privately. After the Test, we were all in the team room and he got up and apologised to us all for the problems he'd caused and explained why he'd done it. But I don't think he apologised for the remarks or said he hadn't meant what he said. He just admitted the timing was probably not right.

That tour was the first time I'd spent any time with Dawson and I found him really honest and a top guy. It's amazing the preconceptions you have about people until you get to know them. A lot of Welsh people probably hated Dawson and Austin Healey at the time. I was guilty of it myself, if I'm being honest. You played against them and they really got on your nerves, because they seem so cocky. So going out on tour, I thought they were going to be really arrogant people.

But I couldn't have been more wrong. They really surprised me. They were two brilliant guys, really good people with a great sense of humour. Dallaglio was another top guy. When you actually got in with them and put your prejudices to one side, you realised you were a great bunch of boys and great characters. At the end of the day, they were rugby players just like you.

The Englishman I became closest to on the trip was Greening, who I'd played age group rugby against as a teenager. I roomed with him that first week in Hampshire and I got on really well with him straight away. He is a real jack-the-lad character and, for the first few weeks, he was the star of the show and great for morale, before his tour was unfortunately cut short by injury.

Jason Leonard was another English guy I really got on with. He was an absolute legend, a player who had done it all, but he was the most down-to-earth bloke you could ever wish to meet and was great fun to be with. I remember his whole thing throughout the tour was trying not to sound Welsh when saying my middle name of Elwyn, which is virtually impossible. He used to love that, a real cockney guy trying to say Elwyn. He was a top bloke.

As for the rugby, I felt things had gone really well for me in the first few weeks of the tour, especially the second game against a Queensland Presidents' XV in Townsville, where Colin Charvis and myself both went well in the back row in a 83–6 demolition.

But I still couldn't believe it when I was named on the bench for the first Test against the Wallabies at the Gabba in Brisbane. I thought I would just be a midweek player so to be in the twenty-two was amazing.

It was a great occasion, with the stadium packed with Lions fans, and it was an awesome win, with Jason Robinson, Dafydd James, Brian O'Driscoll and Scott Quinnell all touching down in a 29–13 victory. We carved the Aussies up that night and O'Driscoll, the Irish centre, was just magnificent. I can still remember our supporters singing 'Waltzing O'Driscoll' to the tune of 'Waltzing Matilda'.

The boys were absolutely bouncing afterwards and

rightly so because it was a fantastic performance. The only disappointment for me was that I hadn't managed to get on the field. We were winning by so much and I was just praying to get on for the last couple of minutes, but it wasn't to be, which was obviously frustrating.

As it turned out, I was to sit on the bench for the final two Tests without getting on as well, but that was probably just as well. By then, my shoulder was absolutely wrecked.

I damaged it against the ACT Brumbies in the midweek match in Canberra after the first Test. Their scrum-half tackled me from behind early on and I couldn't brace myself with my hand so my right shoulder smashed into the ground. I knew something bad had happened, but we were down to our bare bones at the time because we'd had so many injuries. Martin Johnson, the tour captain, was on the bench and they really didn't want to bring him on and risk him getting crocked. So the physios just told me to dig in. They gave me some painkillers at half-time, but I knew I just didn't want to tackle anybody. I didn't want my shoulder to get hit.

I went for an x-ray that night and nothing showed up on it and, to be honest, I don't think they wanted me to go for a scan. So it was a case of more painkillers and get on with it. I was named on the bench for the second Test in Melbourne and I remember hitting the scrummaging machine just prior to that and I knew the shoulder was wrecked. But you are still holding on because you think it might be your only chance to get a Lions Test cap. That didn't happen in the end and I watched on from the bench as we lost those last two Tests.

I've got mixed emotions about the whole experience. Before the first Test, I was just over the moon to get on the bench and be part of the twenty-two. Then, after the final Test, I was gutted, having being so close and yet not getting on to the field. But I'm glad now I didn't go on because my shoulder was in bits and I would have had to come straight back off. I wasn't the only player in pieces by that stage and I think the early part of the tour caught up with us in the end.

It is a difficult balancing act. Coaches are under pressure and they want to make sure they tick all their boxes and do everything they feel is right. But you've got to remember you are dealing with people who have been playing rugby for nine months non-stop and you are also dealing with quality players who don't have to do certain things in training.

You wouldn't be there if you couldn't tackle or couldn't clean people out of a ruck. You've got to trust the players and trust the talent they've got. You are not on a Lions tour to learn things. The biggest thing should be getting the boys to gel together and get to know each other, because you have such a short amount of time to do that.

I think that 2001 tour took a toll on Graham. He copped so much flak he was a different man when he came back. He had been on a hiding to nothing: he wasn't British and, when we lost the series 2–1, it was dubbed a big failure.

With England having had such a good side at the time and with so many quality players in the squad, it was thought we should have done a lot better. Everyone was measuring it against 1997 and the previous trip to Australia in 1989, both of which had been winning tours.

Looking back now, it wasn't as bad a tour as everyone made out at the time and especially not compared to the next Lions trip four years later. We won the first Test in style. We were on top for the first half of the second Test, until Richard Hill got injured, and we only lost the third Test by a six-point margin.

We had nothing left in the tank by the end of the trip. The games had been really intense and had come thick and fast. But the biggest problem was that we had just been overworked in training. That caught up with us in the end. We had been flogged to death.

Given how close we came, despite being on our knees by the end, you can't help but look back on that trip and think of it as a missed opportunity.

# striking a deal

**G**oing on tour with Wales is always an experience, but going on tour a day late is something else again – especially when it's because of a players' strike.

2003 had already been a traumatic year for Welsh rugby. We had suffered a whitewash in the Six Nations, losing all five championship matches to finish rock bottom of the table. And it had also been a troubled time off the field, with endless arguments over the switch to regional rugby – a radical move away from the old club-based system which divided the country and provoked a huge amount of controversy.

One of the reasons for this move to five regional sides was that Welsh rugby was facing financial problems and could no longer sustain nine professional clubs. The Welsh Rugby Union was something like £60m in debt as a result of building the Millennium Stadium and they had brought in a hard-nosed chief executive by the name of David Moffett to try and balance the books. It wasn't long before his attention turned to the players' wage bill.

During Graham Henry's time as national coach, a system had been put in place, which, if the truth be told, meant the boys were probably being overpaid, given the financial position of the WRU. When you played for Wales under Graham you got hugely rewarded. At times it seemed over the top, especially when you were missing out on it!

For the November Test series in 2000, the Wales boys were on £5,000 a win and they had that for beating America and a third-string Samoan team. While they were picking up easy money, I was with Wales A taking on South Africa and New Zealand A, sides full of Super 14 players and future Test stars like Victor Matfield, Jerry Collins, Chris Jack and Keven Mealamu.

Those were two of the toughest matches I'd ever played in and we were really battered and bruised after them. They were far harder than the games the senior side got their big win bonuses for and yet we were only on £250 a game. I remember Stephen Jones going home with minus, once he'd had ticket money and tax deducted!

But by the spring of 2003, Moffett had decided it was time for belts to be tightened across the board. He had appointed a general manager by the name of Steve Lewis, who was handed the task of presenting the Welsh squad members with a new pay deal.

I'll never forget the meeting where Steve first introduced himself to us. It was in a hotel in Tenby down in West Wales, where we used to train some weeks. He came into the room and said: 'The only one of you that will probably understand me here is Mark Taylor.'

Everyone knew Mark was a bright lad who was

qualified as an accountant and it was as if this bloke was saying the rest of us were thick. Now I have got to know Steve quite well since then and he's told me he meant it in jest, but it didn't come across that way at all. So he got off on the wrong footing with us straight away.

And things didn't get any better when he laid out the new pay structure. As with any business deal, he started off low with his opening gambit. That didn't go down too well at all. There were a lot of issues we were unhappy with. It was the whole structure really, although obviously the pay was a big part of it.

The WRU was massively in debt over the stadium, a new regime had come in to try and sort it out and we felt the first ones they were looking at to take the cut were the players. You still had your coaches on £200,000 or whatever they were on a year. We felt we were the ones who were being squeezed ... and we weren't happy.

A stalemate developed, with no agreement being reached, and all the while the summer tour to Australia and New Zealand was drawing ever nearer.

It was never our intention to go on strike. That didn't enter our thoughts until the day we were due to leave. We were supposed to meet up at the team hotel at the Vale of Glamorgan to get the bus down to Heathrow. But we had all spoken to each other on the phone and said we weren't going to the hotel until the WRU agreed to a deal we were satisfied with. So we met up in the Cardiff West service station instead.

Our players' union representative, Richard Harry, who had been handling the negotiations, was actually getting married at the time, so the former Wales skipper Scott

Quinnell took over and was representing the players that day. We agreed that until the WRU reached a deal with Scott and we got the phone call, we were not going.

I remember Gavin Henson and Jonathan Thomas had been called up to the squad as last-minute replacements and they had both gone to the hotel not knowing what was going on and they were the only ones there. The poor kids didn't have a clue what was happening.

Meanwhile, we were all huddled round in the car park at the services, but then we got wind that the press and the management knew where we were, so we moved to the Village Hotel, one junction further down the M4. It was like something out of a comedy, as we all headed off in convoy, except this was no laughing matter.

There wasn't so much a split in our camp, but different people did have different opinions. You had the boys who felt we shouldn't be doing it and that we were going to be condemned if we did. Then there was the more militant side of the squad, the guys that were saying we had to stand by our principles.

I was one of four captains chosen for the tour and I felt very mixed emotions. On the one hand, I could see we were going to get slaughtered for holding out for more money, but it was also the principle of the matter.

Our coaches at the time, Steve Hansen and Scott Johnson, have since said that's the day they realised how tight we were as a group of players. We were a young squad, but a lot of the younger lads were saying we'll stick by this and we'll see it out.

Eventually Scott came down and said, 'Boys you've got to go because the shit's going to hit the fan.'

The WRU had agreed to a certain number of our requirements, while there were others they said they would iron out. So we jumped on the bus and headed up to Heathrow. But it was too late. We had missed our flight and we had to stay in a hotel overnight. That's when things started to get a bit crazy.

You can imagine the phone calls and the texts the boys were getting from back home and we realised then what we had done. It was unheard of for a team to be a day late going out on tour and especially through going on strike. It was a very serious thing.

We knew exactly what the public and the press would be saying. The way they'd see it was that we'd refused to go and represent our country abroad because we wanted more money. We were going to be hung out to dry and accused of bringing shame on the nation. It wasn't as if we were the most popular team at the time anyway, having picked up the wooden spoon in the Six Nations.

We had to pay for our own rooms that night and I felt sorry for our team manager, Alan Phillips, because it must have been a logistical nightmare to have changed all the flights.

Not that the delay meant we had a day off training. Our Kiwi fitness coach, Andrew Hore, never missed an opportunity and he wasn't going to let us off now. There's a big long road outside Heathrow and he had us doing shuttle runs up and down there. People must have been wondering what the hell was going on.

All in all, it wasn't a great couple of days and it didn't paint Welsh rugby in a very good light. But the one positive was that we stayed tight through it all and that bond was to serve us well in the long run.

We eventually flew out a day late and arrived at our training base in North Harbour in New Zealand. A few days later, Steve Lewis came out to talk to the players.

It was a pretty frosty meeting. He wasn't a popular figure with the boys at all at that time, especially after his initial introduction to us. We felt he wasn't giving anything towards us negotiation-wise. The boys didn't take too kindly to him being out there and it was a difficult time for him.

That 2003 trip was a pretty turbulent affair all round. Having travelled out under a cloud we came home under one as well after being smashed 55–3 by the All Blacks in Hamilton. That's not the only time I've been on the receiving end on tour either, both with Wales and the Lions.

But, nevertheless, I've gained a huge amount from the whole touring experience over the years and feel fortunate to have seen so much of the world through rugby. I have always loved travelling and seeing other countries and rugby has enabled me to do that. I've been to Australia, New Zealand, South Africa, Zimbabwe and Argentina, plus Uruguay, Japan and Dubai when I was with the Wales Sevens team early on in my career. I found those Sevens trips did me the world of good as a youngster. They were real eye-openers. To play against some of the top New Zealanders and see how they trained was invaluable.

The one place I've never been on tour is the USA, which is ironic because I go there most years on holiday.

I didn't get picked when Wales went there in 1997, with Gwyn Jones and Rob Appleyard being the two No. 7s ahead of me. Then, in 2005, the Lions tour meant I missed out again.

Away from rugby, I've been to America loads of time. I've been to Vegas, Miami, Los Angeles and New York. Before we had the kids it's where we always used to go on holidays. I love the place and I would emigrate there if I had the chance. Yet I've never had the chance to go there to play rugby, and all the boys who've been say it's the best place you can tour.

The first senior tour I went on with Wales was to Zimbabwe and South Africa in 1998. I found Zimbabwe really interesting. I'd never been anywhere like it before in my life and it was a real cultural experience. I remember there was a flea market next to the hotel and before we left the boys were haggling for ornaments and things. Not that they intended handing over any cash. On the day we were leaving all you could see was the market traders wearing Wales T-shirts and track-suits!

Of all the countries I've toured, Australia is the one I've enjoyed the most. I didn't get to see a whole lot of it in 2001 with the Lions, but when I went back there for the 2003 World Cup I saw a lot more of the place. We were based in Canberra, which probably isn't the ideal tourist destination, but we also went to Melbourne, Sydney and Brisbane and got to spend some time looking around.

A lot of the time on tour you don't see as much of the country as you'd like, because a lot of it is just going from hotel to training pitch. But that was the brilliant thing about going on tour with Steve Hansen and Scott

Johnson. They always had the balance right and you always had time off to go and see the country as well. They realised that's what touring is all about – it's about getting the whole experience. That's why that 2003 World Cup trip stands out as the best tour I've been on.

In contrast, while I wouldn't say New Zealand was a disappointment, I did find it a bit intense on the 2005 Lions tour. It was just 24/7 rugby and you couldn't get away from it, because it was on TV and in the papers the whole time.

In 2001 in Australia, nobody really noticed the Lions were there until the first Test match. But from the minute we landed in New Zealand it was front page, back page wherever we went and we didn't see anywhere near as much of the country as we would have liked.

Apparently it's a really nice country outside of the cities, but all we saw were the cities and the training grounds. It was a shame we didn't get to see more of the place. The Kiwis I know talk about some great places over there and I know people who went there to watch the Lions who travelled around a bit, had a great time and said it's a beautiful place. So I'd like to go back there purely for a holiday and also get the chance to see it that way.

Tours have changed quite a bit over my career. On my first one with Wales to South Africa in 1998 we played a load of midweek games, but that's all gone now. You have two Test matches and that's it. The trips are a lot more professional now as well. You speak to ex-players about their tours in years gone by and it's a million miles away from what we have now. The old tours were more or less a three-week holiday.

Mind you, you would still get some old-school tourists in the modern era, like Chris Wyatt, the former Llanelli second row. He was always good fun on tour and he only seemed to need about two hours' sleep a night. The Wales physio Mark Davies – or Carcass as we know him – is always a really good tourist, too. He's old school and he's always got a story to tell whatever country you're in.

And you do still get the famous players' courts from time to time. We had one at the 2003 World Cup on the last day before we came home, after we'd lost to England in the quarter-finals. Robin McBryde and I organised it: Robin was the judge and I was his helper. There were a few people up for various crimes and misdemeanours, like Ceri Sweeney, who had actually booked his holiday for the semi-final weekend. He took a lot of stick for that in court. We dressed him up in a pair of Speedos and put false tan over him and got him a rubber ring and a Spanish hat!

There may have been really good memories along the way, but from the playing side, end-of-season tours are always difficult. You are coming off the back of nine months of hard rugby and have to dig deep for one last effort. To make matters worse, you are up against sides that are fresh and at the peak of their fitness.

Ideally, to my mind, everyone's season should start and finish at the same time, in both the northern and southern hemispheres. And if you want to get the best out of players, I think you should have a maximum of twenty-five games per season.

Obviously that's a difficult one because the games have got to be played to bring revenue in and keep things going. But if the seasons ran side by side, in north and south, it would make life so much easier.

Logically, that would mean summer rugby, with a global season running from February to October. It would be the same as you have now in terms of overall length, just at a different time of the year.

I know that would be huge cultural change and a lot of people would probably oppose the idea. But if the game's going to move forward it's something that's got to happen. It's been adopted in rugby league and has improved their game no end. I think it could do the same for us.

I'm pretty certain crowds would go up for one thing. It's always nicer to watch sport in nice weather than on a freezing cold, wet day. In Australia they've got the weather and they make a whole day of it.

The pitches would be better as well and the game would naturally become a yard or two yards faster. It would be more entertaining and more people would want to come and watch it.

The biggest thing I found when touring New Zealand and Australia was the quality of the pitches. When I was with the Lions in New Zealand, we played against Manawatu, who are one of the smaller provincial teams and we smashed them. But the surface of that pitch was as good as anything I've ever played on in the northern hemisphere. There are so few good surfaces around in the UK. It would make such a difference if they were better and summer rugby is the way to ensure that.

But whatever the future I hope there is still room for tours in the schedule. I feel very fortunate when I think about the places rugby has taken me and it would be sad if future players missed out on that experience.

When you are a professional, and especially if you take it seriously, you do miss out on a lot of things, both with your friends and socially. You've got to sacrifice a lot, but on the other hand you get to travel first class around the world, you stay in the best hotels and are really well looked after, with everything being done for you. I savour it a lot more now than I used to. I used to take it for granted when I was younger. Now I go to these places and I really try and take it in. I realise how lucky I am and what a privilege it is and how it's not going to last.

Some boys don't like being away from home. For me travelling has been one of the perks of the job. It has been difficult being away for a long time since I've had a family, but when you are younger it's one of the best experiences you can ever have. I feel very grateful for what the game has given me on that front.

## chapter 12

# hello mr hansen

I've become used to the idea of my international hopes resting in the hands of various Welsh coaches over the years, but what I'll never forget is the day the fate of one of those men lay in mine.

It was August 2003 and Wales had just suffered a humiliating 43–9 defeat to an English second string at the Millennium Stadium. That was our tenth loss in a row and there was a lot of flak flying in the direction of our Kiwi coach Steve Hansen. We'd been whitewashed in the Six Nations and now we'd been thumped by what was effectively England B, despite having our strongest team out. The whole country was in mourning.

In fact I was just about the only person with anything to be happy about because after that game Steve had told me I was going to be captain for the World Cup, which I was really chuffed about at the time.

Then, the following evening, he rang me up at home and asked if I could go back up to the Vale of

Glamorgan Hotel, where he was staying. I thought that was a bit strange and wondered if he'd changed his mind about the captaincy.

So I went to his room not really knowing what to expect, but what he said took my breath away. Without any beating about the bush, he just said: 'If I've lost the changing room, I'll resign tomorrow.'

It was the first time I'd ever been confronted with anything like that and I was really shocked. It was surreal to think that the future of the Wales coach depended on what I said next.

Now you have to understand that I wasn't really the biggest fan of the guy at the time and here was my chance to get rid of him. But I couldn't lie. The truth was that he hadn't lost the boys at all and I told him as much. So he stayed and the rest is history as they say. Looking back, I shudder to think what would have happened to Welsh rugby if I'd taken that opportunity to help show him the door.

Steve Hansen first arrived in Wales just before Christmas 2001. He'd been brought in from Canterbury by Graham Henry to take over as forwards coach from Lynn Howells, although he'd actually been an inside-centre as a player as we found out later.

He didn't arrive with anything like the fanfare that had greeted Henry and I can't say he made a big first impression on me. I was recovering from the shoulder injury I'd picked up on the Lions tour at the time and was doing some weights in the gym when I first met him. He came over and mumbled something to me, as he does in his own way.

To start with, he stayed very much in the background but then, when Graham resigned after we were thumped by Ireland in the opening game of the 2002 Six Nations, all that changed. All of a sudden, we had this new guy thrust in as head coach and we didn't know a thing about him.

His first game in charge was against France at the Millennium Stadium. Before you leave the hotel to go to the ground, you always have a meeting where the coach gives you your final team talk. Well Hansen's first one was a bit different. We were all sitting in there and suddenly the door opens, he walks in with a glass in his hand and throws it at the wall, smashing it everywhere. We were all thinking, 'What the hell is this?' and he came out with something like, 'If you're not tight today, that's exactly what's going to happen to us, we are going to shatter into pieces.'

Up to then, he'd remained pretty much behind the scenes and no one really knew what to expect from him. So that was a case of 'Welcome to Mr Hansen'.

It proved a great game against the French. We played really well and could well have won it, with Scott Quinnell and Dafydd James both going agonisingly close to scoring. Although we lost in the end, it brought a bit of pride back into everyone, because we had been on a downer since losing at home to Argentina in the autumn and then getting smashed out in Dublin.

The feel-good factor continued when we beat Italy in our next game, but then we came down to a earth with a bump when we were hammered at Twickenham and lost at home to Scotland. So any kind of honeymoon period was soon over for the new coach. But he was already looking at the much bigger picture – and he had big plans.

I'll be honest, I didn't like him at first. I had been in the Wales set-up for five or six years and I was a bit stuck in my ways and thought I knew it all. I'd been on a Lions tour, I was first choice in the team and I probably thought I was better than I was. Then this guy comes in and starts to change everything.

Graham had basically stuck with the same team for most of his time in charge. But Hansen had obviously been sitting behind the scenes, looking at what was going on, and when he took over he decided the whole place needed a shake-up. He felt it needed some young, fresh blood and he wasn't afraid to make changes or to drop the bigger names; people who thought they were guaranteed their places in the side. He immediately weaned out the players he thought weren't pulling their weight and who he thought were only there for the glory of it all.

Off the field, the changes were even more dramatic. He was one of these guys who was huge on values and he imposed them with a rod of iron. He was red hot on dress code and there were little things, like you couldn't wear a cap or flip-flops at dinner. It was like nothing we'd ever experienced before and a lot of the senior players couldn't buy into it. In the Henry era, things like that weren't looked at at all. It was all about what happened on the field.

But with Steve, the off-the-field stuff was just as important and with him it was very much a case of my way or the highway. So when we found out that he used to be a policeman, we weren't really that surprised. You could definitely see that he was an ex-copper from the way he laid down the law. Once a policeman always a policeman and that was something Dafydd James, the Wales and Lions winger, was to learn to his cost.

One of the biggest changes Steve made was that we had to stay in at the Vale of Glamorgan Hotel the whole time we were in camp. We weren't allowed out home at all. That led to the press dubbing it the Jail of Glamorgan and at times it did feel a bit like a jail. It was when Daf made a 'jail-break' that he famously fell foul of PC Hansen. He only lives down the road and he decided to go home for the night. He was back at the Vale by 7.30 in the morning, but it was his bad luck that Steve happened to be going out for a walk just as he was coming in.

Steve asked him where he'd been and I think Daf said he'd been to get some DVDs from his car. But, being a typical copper, Steve went to his car and felt the exhaust pipe and saw that it was still warm. Now who else would have thought of that apart from Hansen? But Daf had been caught and he ended up getting suspended for a match.

In hindsight, you can see where Steve was coming from. In truth, it was like a holiday camp when Graham was in charge. His attitude was that we were adults and we could look after ourselves. But I think we had ended up being given too much slack and had started to take everything for granted. We had got in a comfort zone. Steve could see that and decided to do something about it. It makes sense now, but at the time it didn't go down well with a lot of the players, especially the ones who had been around for a while.

When you've got a group of players who are used to doing things a certain way, your initial reaction when someone comes in and changes everything is resentment and you question why they are doing it. It's the way we are.

It's tough because you know what's made you successful as a player and it's very hard to change. In Wales, we are a difficult race to change in our ways and our thoughts. Steve came in and tried to revamp everything on and off the field. It was like reinventing the wheel. Having been part of the Henry era, I didn't like the changes one bit to start with. And, I must admit, he really got to me at times.

That first summer, in 2002, we went on tour to South Africa. I was the first-choice seven at the time and, although you never take it for granted, I was pretty confident of my place. But I remember him coming up to me before the first Test and saying: 'You're picked for this game, but you're lucky.' That was Steve all over. You never sat easy with the guy.

I found it really hard to deal with for a long time and I resented him so much for the first eighteen months of his coaching reign. You only have to ask my wife how many times I went home and said: 'I hate him.' He frustrated me so much. You could sit and have a tidy chat with him and think he's a really nice guy and then he'd do things that would drive you mad. But it was all just to do with getting you out of your comfort zone. I can appreciate that now, but at the time it was hard to get your head round.

As if Hansen wasn't enough of a culture shock, we also had to get to grips with another character from Down Under, Scott Johnson.

Johnno – as he came to be known to all of us – came in to help Steve with the backs after Graham left and you can just imagine our first impressions of the guy. We'd never seen anyone like him before. He was a cross between Gerard Depardieu, with his long hair, and some kind of tanned surfer dude. And you just couldn't shut him up.

He came in and he was your typical brash Aussie. He upset a lot of the boys initially when, the first time he came to training, he said: 'When's the senior side coming out?' He looked at us from a conditioning point of view and thought: 'God, this is like an Under-20s side.'

We didn't really know what to make of him at first and we were thinking, 'Who's the loud mouth?' With him and Hansen together at the helm, it was a real culture shock for us.

I think they came to the conclusion pretty early on that they had to change the style we were trying to play. Steve had tried to get us playing like Canterbury initially, but we just weren't big enough or fit enough to do that.

The thing about Welsh rugby is we haven't got any monsters here. We've got clever, quick players and that's our strength. Steve and Johnno saw that and decided to develop a style of play that made the most of those strengths.

But at first the boys just couldn't buy into it. We couldn't see where they were coming from or what they wanted to do. We couldn't understand what they were trying to get at basically, either on or off the field. We didn't know what had hit us.

But looking back, it all starts to make sense now. It was on the tour of South Africa in the summer of 2002 that you could see the first signs of what Hansen was trying to do with us. He'd brought a lot of new players in for trip, including a bunch of Pontypridd boys, like Michael Owen, Robert Sidoli and Mefin Davies, with Colin Charvis installed as skipper.

We didn't really know each other as players, so he did little things like split us into groups, give us some money and tell us to organise our own meals that night and to find a restaurant. You also had little competitions in training within your certain teams.

We had never done things like that before and, as the tour went on, we became really close as a group. It just built and built. We did really well on the field as well, played some good stuff and should have beaten South Africa in at least one of the two Tests.

We followed that up with a pretty good autumn, where we stuffed Canada and Fiji and performed okay against New Zealand. We felt we were really progressing and, because I'd been named player of the series, I was feeling a lot happier.

But then came Rome. It was unheard of for Wales to lose to Italy, but that's what happened. It was a huge wake-up call and marked the low point of my career up to then. It was our skipper, Charvy, who ended up getting all the stick for smiling in the dug-out after being taken off. I think it was just the way the camera caught his expression that made it look like he was smiling, but he ended up becoming Public Enemy No. 1.

It was a desperate start to the 2003 Six Nations and things weren't to get any better: we lost all five championship matches. The truth was we were still going through a transitional period and still getting used to the style the coaches wanted us to play. We were also training way more during that campaign than we would normally have done during a Six Nations. That was where Andrew Hore came in.

Hore had worked with Hansen at Canterbury and he'd been brought in as fitness coach the summer before. We'd heard that his nickname was 'Chisel', so were expecting this 6ft 7in guy with rippling muscles. But when he turned up, he was just this little Kiwi. Mind you, he had big ideas.

Just before we left to go to South Africa, he gave us a little bit of a talk and said we would have to come in and train after we came back. We were looking at each other and thinking, 'Are you kidding us. After the tour, it's feet up.'

But he was serious and that was just the beginning. He came in and saw how far behind we were with our conditioning. He then decided to do something about it.

So during that 2003 Six Nations, he had us doing hill runs and things like that on our weeks off, which was very unusual. Looking back now, though, it's clear the coaches were thinking about the World Cup.

They realised they had to get us in condition for that tournament later on in the year and they were prepared to take the hit in terms of results in the meantime and deal with any flak that came their way as a result. That continued to be the policy in the summer – and it almost cost Hansen his job.

We had taken a lot of flak for our performances in the Six Nations and we went out on a very tough tour at the end of the season. In June, we went to Australia and New Zealand, which was always going to be hard, and ended up suffering a record 55–3 defeat to the All Blacks in Hamilton, which earned the coach yet more criticism.

Then, in August, we had a series of World Cup warm-up matches against Ireland, England, Romania and Scotland. Now Hansen & co had a clear plan for that period. They were going to train right through regardless of the games. I remember him sitting the senior players down and explaining the situation. He said he just wanted to play the main group in one game and to really blast the conditioning. They were determined, whatever the cost, to get us fit.

The fact that we had games at the end of the week didn't mean we were going to lay off in training. And, almost inevitably, our performances suffered as result. We lost out in Dublin with a mix-and-match side and then we put our first-choice side out against England's 'seconds' in Cardiff – and got stuffed. It was after that he called me in and asked if he'd lost the boys, but that wasn't the case at all. It was just that we were tired after all the training and hadn't quite clicked yet as we would have liked.

I remember there was so much pressure on him then before the Scotland game in Cardiff the following week. As I understand it, the WRU made it clear to him that if he lost that game he was gone. He had already picked the side and had left out most of the so-called first-choice players to have a look at some squad players ahead of the World Cup. I think the WRU tried to pressure him to change it but, to his credit, he stuck to his guns. It would have been an easy option to change the side and put in the so-called big names to try and save his own neck. But he said no, I've got a long-term plan here and I'm sticking by it.

That period there is when the boys really started to know what he was about and they gained so much respect for him. In fairness to him, he was brilliant when it came to protecting the boys. Despite all the flak flying around, he would take it all on his shoulders and nothing would come back on the players. He would never once look for an out.

The thing that perhaps earned him most criticism was the way he used to go on about performance rather than results and I can see where people found that hard to understand. But he wasn't just saying that to the press, he would say it to the players as well. Time and again he would tell us that if we concentrated on the performance, the result would take care of itself. He said when you are out on the field you should forget about the scoreboard and just make sure you do your next job well.

He kept saying it because he believed it and that's what the guy was all about. If he believed in something he'd keep on doing it, regardless of the consequences for himself. He could have easily buckled under the pressure before that Scotland game, but he stuck by his principles. He put the good of the national side ahead of his job security. He could have easily changed things just for that one game. But no, he was looking at the World Cup and he felt we could be competitive at the World Cup in Australia if he stuck to his plan. And he proved to be dead right.

In the end, we beat Scotland and he kept his job. It's

scary to think about what would have happened to Welsh rugby if we'd lost that game and he'd gone. And it's scary to think what would have happened if I'd given him a different answer in his hotel room that August evening in 2003.

## chapter 13

# the world is watching

Throughout 2003, the message coming out of the Welsh camp had been the same: 'Judge us on the World Cup.' We'd put all the emphasis on preparing for the World Cup and getting in peak condition for that tournament, sometimes at the expense of results along the way. If things went well out in Australia, then the policy would be justified. If we failed, there could be no excuses.

So when we arrived Down Under at the end of September, we knew we had to stand up and be counted. It was judgement time for us as a team. Everything had been geared towards the World Cup and we knew if we didn't get to the quarter-finals we would be slaughtered back home.

So there was a lot of pressure on us, but we were very optimistic. Physically we were in the best nick we'd ever been in and, from day one, training went really well. All the things we'd been working on for the past year or so were starting to come together.

We were also very close as a group by now because of all the tough times we'd been through. There was a real strong team spirit and a good buzz about the camp and that just built up as the days went by. Colin Charvis had been appointed skipper after I turned down the job and, from the moment we got out there, he was brilliant in the role and everyone got behind him.

We were based in Canberra, but not in the usual five-star hotel. We were staying in self-catering apartments, which I think was a really good idea. Sometimes when you are in hotels all the time on tour it gets a bit monotonous, with the same food, and you can easily get bored. Plus you are often sharing a small space with someone else.

In Canberra, we had our own rooms plus a separate lounge and dining room. We could go across the road for a coffee, go to the video shop and we were within walking distance of some nice restaurants. You could also prepare your own food if you wanted to. It was unheard of for an international side to do that, but it was something different and it broke things up.

I was sharing an apartment with Iestyn Harris and let's just say he wasn't the head chef. I don't think cooking was his strong point. He was good at putting dishes in the dishwasher, but that's about it. Steve Hansen was always thinking: having us in those apartments and creating a kind of little community really pulled everyone together early on in that trip.

When we first arrived in Australia, we didn't really feel the atmosphere of the World Cup so much. Everything on TV and in the papers was all geared to the Rugby League grand final. But as the days went by we started to feel the atmosphere build and there was a big shift in focus to the World Cup.

By the time our opening pool match against Canada finally came around, we were just itching to get out there and play. For most of us, our last game had been that humiliating defeat at home to England seven weeks earlier, which was obviously a match to forget. The first thing you want to do when you have a bad performance like that is to play straight away and most of us hadn't had that chance. It had been frustrating not to have been able to make amends. That had been the hardest thing.

I don't normally get anxious before games, but I was really worried going into that Canada match in Melbourne. It was the most nervous I'd ever been before any match. It wasn't just me, either. Most of the other boys felt the same too, because we hadn't played for a while and it was such a massive game for us. There was a lot of pressure. If we'd lost that one, it could have wrecked the whole trip for us.

So we were really relieved to get the win. We played particularly well as a team, while Iestyn had a superb match at inside-centre and showed everyone just how good a player he was. It's difficult when you change codes but, by that time, I felt he had matured into a world-class centre. It was a special performance from him that night. He set the ball rolling with a great break to create our first try from his co-centre Sonny Parker and we didn't look back after that, crossing the line six times in a 41–10 win. We were happy with the result and glad to have got the show back on the road. If there was one word that summed up the mood in the camp it was 'relief'.

But then, in our next pool match against Tonga in a rain-sodden Canberra, we really struggled. I don't know why it is, but we always seem to find it tough against Pacific Island sides. Mind you, the night didn't go too badly for me, as I came off the bench to help secure a 27–20 win by scoring a try out wide and landing a drop goal of all things, which I got a fair bit of stick for because it was a pretty ugly effort.

Then it was the key game against Italy, which we had to win to qualify for the quarter-finals. Looking back, I can honestly say that, in terms of pressure, that match was on a par with the 2005 Grand Slam game against Ireland. At least for the Irish game we were confident. Before Italy we still had doubts in ourselves. We weren't used to winning big pressure games at that time as a group and this was a massive game for us.

But we dealt with the pressure and won 27–15 to gain sweet revenge for the defeat in Rome earlier in the year. We scored three tries, through Sonny, Mark Jones and my fellow flanker Dafydd Jones, but it was our defence that really won the day as we made 174 tackles, a staggering figure.

Once we won that one, it was as if we'd achieved our goal. We knew if we had come home without getting to the quarters we would have been crucified. But now we were through and the pressure was off for our final group game against New Zealand.

It was then that Steve told me he wanted me to have a rest. He said to me and Iestyn that we'd done really well and that he wanted to give the other boys a run. I understood because I had played a part in the first three matches and it wasn't as if I was being dropped. I'd had a good campaign up until then and it was just a case of taking a break before the big one in the quarter-final. I do remember saying to Iestyn, 'We might not get back in,' but it was only jokingly, because to be honest I thought we'd get stuffed by the All Blacks. I honestly did.

The guys who went out on the field that night hadn't really trained together as a group. I remember Shane Williams had been in bed all week with the flu. How he played like he did, I'll never know. It was genius.

That night in Sydney changed Welsh rugby. Gareth Thomas came on at full-back for Garan Evans and that changed his career forever. It was a defining moment for a lot of the other boys, too. Jonathan Thomas was awesome that night, Charvy was brilliant and, of course, it was the night when Shane announced himself to the world.

Steve has since said he picked that team because he felt it was the one that could beat New Zealand, but I think he's putting a bit of spin on it there for the press. Basically, I think it was just a case of him giving the rest of the squad a game before the quarter-finals. No disrespect to those boys, but they knew that themselves. I don't think he could have envisaged in his wildest dreams how well they would play that night. None of us in the squad expected the team to play that well.

So how did it happen? I just think the shackles were off us. We had nothing to lose and the boys just clicked as a group. All that we'd trained for, all that we'd worked on came to fruition that night. We just went out and played and that's when we realised that what we had been working on not only worked, but that it worked against the best side in the world. We ran in four tries and led 34–28 at one stage before eventually going down 53–37 in what most people agree was the match of the tournament.

Sitting up in the stand watching that game was one of the strangest feelings ever. On the one hand, you were so glad for the boys because a lot of them hadn't been given the opportunity before. But it was also a horrible feeling. It was such a special moment and you wanted to be part of it because you'd worked towards it for so long. You also knew in the back of your mind what it might mean for you. When I got back to my room that night, I remember thinking, 'I'm not going to get back in this side.'

After that game, I was speaking to Gareth Llewellyn and we were both saying, 'How can you change that side the way it played?'

But I still obviously hoped I would get the nod for the quarter-final against England. So when Steve said he was sticking with the same side, I was absolutely gutted. Being left out had to rank as the biggest disappointment of my career up to that point. I'd been dropped before, but this was different. I felt my form had been good and that I'd been playing pretty well during the tournament. So it came as a massive blow when Steve pulled me to one side and told me I wasn't going to be in the side. It was such a huge game and I was desperate to play in it.

I was angry and frustrated at first and it took me a

while to come to terms with things. But then, when I sat back and thought about it, I realised that no one is bigger than the team. And how could he change the side anyway when it had produced one of the best nights Wales had had for years? Although we didn't win, it was one of the best performances we'd produced for ages.

Steve told me that if it had been anyone else we were playing then I would have started. He said there was nothing wrong with my form; it was just that he had a particular plan. He wanted to wear England down up front. He said although I'd played well in the early games, for the good of the team this was the best side to play England and keep the ball rolling.

The way the players had performed against New Zealand, I couldn't really argue with him. I would have loved to be out there from the start, because you always want to be part of it, especially a huge game like that, but I just had to swallow it and accept his decision.

I had loads of messages from back home after the team was announced and the players were very supportive as well. And Steve made a special point in the last squad meeting of saying how I'd reacted to it quite well and was fairly philosophical with it all.

Steve initially told me I would come on at half-time, but we were going so well he kept Jonathan Thomas on after the break. To be honest, the game was so exciting I got a bit carried away with it and forgot that I might be going on. I was just like a spectator cheering on the team, especially when we scored those two first-half tries through Stephen Jones and Charvy.

Our confidence going into that game in Brisbane was so

high and we really felt we could win – and at half-time we were on course to do just that. There were stacks of English in the stadium, but you could sense their frustration. We had less fans than them, but the support we had was still brilliant.

In the end, I came on for the last twenty-five minutes after England had turned the game round, and I was lucky enough to score another try. After waiting more than thirty caps to get one, they were suddenly starting to come thick and fast. It was a lovely cross-kick from Ceri Sweeney and Shane Williams did a great job in competing with Lawrence Dallaglio which, in terms of height, should have been a no-contest. All I had to do was fall on the ball. That score put us back in contention, but there was too much ground to make up. The damage had been done in the first fifteen minutes after half-time.

England had changed their gameplan, with Mike Catt coming on having made a big difference. They started kicking to the corners, played territory well and Jonny Wilkinson kicked his goals after Jason Robinson had produced a bit of magic to put Will Greenwood over. But to outscore them by three tries to one was a big plus and we were able to hold our heads up high at the final whistle.

Looking back, I don't resent Steve at all for not picking me. He had a job to do and he made what he felt was the right decision for the side at the time.

There was an amazing atmosphere in the team hotel after the match, with loads of Welsh supporters in there. They seemed really pleased with our efforts and the players were really happy with the way they'd performed. The big thing was that we hadn't just gone out and dug in. We'd played some really good, attractive rugby and were hailed as the surprise package of the tournament. Welsh rugby was back.

We had taken a lot of flak during 2003 and maybe rightly so. But we had been telling everyone to judge us on the World Cup and during the tournament we showed we weren't a bad side.

Before we headed home, we had a team meeting where Steve said we had to build on what we'd achieved and to take things to the next level. Colin reiterated that message straight away.

So that was the target going into the 2004 Six Nations and, in our opening game against Scotland, we carried on from where we had left off in Australia and played a really expansive game, with Rhys Williams touching down twice on the wing in a 23–10 victory.

But then we came back down to earth with a bump against Ireland in Dublin, losing 36–15. I was captain for that one because Colin was injured and we decided to play against the wind in the first half. The Irish killed us for that decision. They scored a couple of tries really early on with the wind and we could never get into the game after that. I remember myself, Alfie, Stephen Jones and Steve discussing it before the game and we decided then to go against the wind. With hindsight you should always play with it at Lansdowne Road and not let Ireland get their tails up.

It was a frustrating campaign. We played well against both France and England without getting the results. What made it all the more frustrating was that Steve Hansen was going back to New Zealand at the end of the championship and we wanted to send him off on a winning note. At least we were able to do that with our final game against Italy, where we cruised home 44–10.

However well we'd done in the World Cup, Steve wasn't the public's No. 1 figure. They didn't really warm to him as a person and didn't like the way he harped on about performance. But when you saw the ovation he had from the boys at the end of that Italy game and the way we all clapped him in when he walked off the pitch, it showed just how much we thought of him. It was quite emotional.

But even then, I don't think we realised just how good a job he'd done. It's only since he's gone that we've really appreciated all the things he put in place for us. Every passing month you realise more and more what he and Johnno did for us.

They were really the perfect coaching combination. It was good cop, bad cop with them. Looking back it was brilliant. They were so clever. Hansen would be the bad cop and then Johnno would be the one all the boys would go and speak to. He served as the eyes of the operation. It worked really well.

You could also have a flat-out argument with either of them and know there would be no grudges held. Apparently they were like that to each other as well. Behind closed doors they would rip each other to shreds then, once they had walked out of the room, it was forgotten. Nothing was personal.

I'll be the first to admit that, initially, I couldn't understand where they were coming from as coaches. But the longer you were there, the more you realised what they were trying to do. They were all about developing the individual. Hansen pulled in a lot of young kids he saw potential in and spent time developing them. He was willing to sacrifice the wins in the process, even when it meant putting his own job at risk.

He was one of the shrewdest men you've ever seen and realised we needed to start from scratch again if we were to re-establish ourselves as a force. We might have been holding our own in the Six Nations, but on a world level we were way behind. Coming from a set-up like Canterbury he could see that and he knew he had to change everything both on and off the field. He developed us so much mentally and as players. He gave people opportunities they would never have had under a more conservative coach and developed so many of the boys who went on to become Lions.

To me the success New Zealand are having now is no accident. Henry and Hansen are probably the perfect combination. Graham is so thorough and nothing is left to chance, while Steve would be on the players' backs all the time. It doesn't matter who they are, none of them would be able to get in the comfort zone and he'll be challenging them constantly. That was the thing with Hansen. You never sat easy when he was around and you became a better player as a result.

As for Johnno, he initially just came across as this stereotypical, brash, Aussie know-all that thought he was an expert on everything. But, as time went on, it became obvious that he really did know his stuff. He was such a technical coach. He would sit us down and analyse games and explain to us what was happening in a way we'd never been shown before. He revolutionised the way we saw the game.

In British rugby it's too much a case of saying to the forwards, 'You do your scrum, your line-outs, you do your smashing.' As forwards under Hansen and Johnson, we would do as much ball-handling in training as the backs. There would be specific times when you'd join in with the backs. We had never done that before. Normally the backs would be doing all the handling skills and we'd be doing all the head-down stuff. That's the biggest change Johnno brought in from my point of view and, of course, everyone in the backs idolised him.

Andrew Hore was as big an influence as the two of them. He was just on a different level to anyone we'd ever had. Mind you, he was the bane of your life. I'd have a day off from Cardiff and he'd say: 'Right, we can get a speed session in here or an extra weights session.' It was as if I never had a day off. But I would have been finished by 2002 if it hadn't been for him. When it came to conditioning, the game was moving on at a rate of knots and if Horey hadn't been there, a lot of us would have stayed in our comfort zones and fallen miles behind.

As a trio, they were just so committed. You'd go past their offices up at the indoor barn at the Vale of Glamorgan at 10pm at night and the lights would still be on. They'd still be working. So it wasn't just a case of them telling us to put the hours in, they were actually doing it themselves. Their work ethic was incredible.

I don't think Welsh rugby has come close to realising what those three did for it. The only ones who will ever really appreciate what they did are the players who were involved in those three years. You speak to any of those boys and, to a man, they will all speak really highly of them. We can't use enough superlatives to describe how influential they were on us and how they changed the work ethic and the standards of the squad.

They are, without a doubt, the best coaches I've ever worked under as a group. It's strange saying that now, given that we lost ten in a row in 2003, but I think they did a great job in really difficult circumstances and with the structure of Welsh rugby being up in the air.

They went back to the start and rebuilt everything, both on and off the field. They instilled values in us, developed a great team spirit and got us playing a style of rugby that made the best use of our strengths as players. It's ironic that it took three men from the other side of the world to get us playing a traditional Welsh brand of rugby again. They made us grow as a group of players.

And all that led to the 2005 Grand Slam.

## chapter 14

# we're on the way to slam-arillo

If ever you needed proof of the part fate can play in sport, then look no further than my 2005 Six Nations campaign.

I ended up winning the Grand Slam with Wales and being named player of the championship – and yet it could all have been so different. In fact, at one stage, I wondered whether I was going to play any part in the tournament at all.

At the start of the year, the best I thought I could hope for was a place on the bench. After all, that was the role I'd occupied throughout the autumn internationals, with Colin Charvis monopolising the No. 7 jersey.

It was frustrating, because you always want to start, but I couldn't really complain because the side was going so well, pushing both South Africa and New Zealand right to the wire, and at least I came on in all the games.

But, just a few days into the New Year, it looked as though I was going to be denied even the sub's role. It was early January and I was in the gym at the David Lloyd Centre in Cardiff doing a 7.30am weights session.

Now I hate doing weights that early in the morning, but this session was to prove even more unpleasant than usual. I was doing a push-press and something just gave way in my neck. I couldn't get in my car after that and I was in agony all day. I'd never felt a pain like it before and I knew it was something more than just a pulled muscle.

I sat out the rest of that month, missing two or three games, but it still wouldn't settle down, so I was sent for a scan. I still think of what happened next to this day.

It was just over two weeks before the start of the Six Nations and the Wales physio Mark 'Carcass' Davies pulled me in and said they'd had the results of the scan. He told me I had a partially prolapsed disc and there was no way I would be fit for the first two games against England and Italy. I was absolutely devastated.

But that's when fate took a hand. That weekend, Charvy was playing for Newcastle against the Newport-Gwent Dragons in a Heineken Cup match and badly injured his foot. A couple of days later I went into the Welsh camp and I can still remember Carcass saying: 'We'd better get a second opinion on that neck of yours.' So we went to see the specialist and he scanned it again. It was still only 50-50, but at least now I had half a chance.

The talk in the press was that either Robin Sowden-Taylor or Richie Pugh were going to start on the open-side against England. But, behind the scenes, they were pulling out all the stops to try and get me fit – with the Cardiff masseur, Wayne Mortimer, playing a huge part –

and they gave me until the Wednesday before the game to do some contact work. The truth was I wouldn't have even been on the bench if Charvy hadn't been crocked but, with him out, they felt they needed that experience. It's fair to say there was a dramatic turnaround in my condition once Colin got injured!

My neck was still quite painful initially, but it gradually got better as the days went by and, if anything, once I did that contact work on the Wednesday it kind of clicked back into place and cleared up. It wasn't exactly a medical miracle, but it wasn't too far short of it.

There's a saying that one man's despair is another man's fortune and that was certainly the case on this occasion. Charvy had been outstanding in the autumn and was being talked of as a certainty for the Lions. The odds on him picking up such a freakish injury at that exact moment must have been 100–1. But, all of a sudden he was out, I was somehow fit and the rest, as they say, is history.

I couldn't have scripted the opening game of the championship any better from a personal point of view. It was my fiftieth cap and leading Wales out that day against England at the Millennium Stadium stands out as the proudest moment of my career, more so than being captain.

If someone had told me when I was fourteen or fifteen that I would get fifty caps, I would never have believed them. For that to fall in to place with England at home in the first game of the Six Nations was a dream come true. Tanni Grey, the great wheelchair athlete, was the team mascot that day and my mother was there as well, so it was an emotional time. To cap it all with an 11–9 win just made it the perfect day.

I had never beaten England before, but we felt we had come on loads as a squad over the previous eighteen months and we were definitely confident. So were the public. Everyone kind of expected us to win, which was unusual for us against England and it's a situation we don't handle very well sometimes.

There was also a big question mark over whether we had the mental toughness to actually beat a big side. We had come close to beating both South Africa and New Zealand in the autumn, but we hadn't quite been able to finish them off. So, although we had the confidence, we hadn't experienced the big win as yet; that breakthrough moment. We hadn't beaten one of the top five nations for a really long time.

It looked as though it was going to be another case of so near, yet so far when England went ahead with about ten minutes to go. But that was the cue for 'Gav's kick'.

As soon as Gavin Henson stepped up to take that match-winning penalty, I never doubted he would make it given the form he was in at the time and the mentality he's got. I don't think he ever doubted himself either. It changed his life really and it was the first step towards changing all of our lives: it kick-started the whole thing.

It wasn't a classic game by any means, but it was a breakthrough moment for us. We had finally claimed that big scalp. Admittedly, England were in a transitional period themselves and had lost a few key players, but to beat them at any time is an achievement and it was really important for us as a squad, because it was our first big win. We'd been through a lot of tough times together and now all our hard work had finally been rewarded. We were on our way.

Nevertheless, none of us in the squad believed we were going to win the Grand Slam. It was Italy away next and most of us had been out to Rome two years earlier and lost, so we weren't about to get carried away with anything. We knew how tough it was going to be and there were still a lot of wounds open from 2003.

Initially, I thought I was going to miss the game because I'd hurt my knee in the first ten minutes against England. I had a scan on it afterwards and on the Monday the specialist said I probably wouldn't be fit for Italy. But once again my body wasn't about to listen to reason and I found myself on the pitch in Rome.

We made a good start with a try from Jonathan Thomas, but then they hit back with an interception and I thought to myself this is going to be really tough. But that was the game where we really clicked and started playing well and we went on to record a comfortable 38–8 victory.

I scored just before half-time, when I managed to dab the ball onto the bottom of the post, and that gave us a bit of breathing space. There was no looking back after that and we scored six tries in all, including a great one from Shane Williams, where Gareth Thomas launched a counter and myself and Kevin Morgan both popped passes up off the floor. I think that's the best try we scored all season and it just summed up what we are about really, always looking to attack and keep the ball alive.

There was a great mood in the dressing room afterwards. Tony Christie's song 'Show me the way to

Amarillo' was a big hit at the time and we had that blasting out. It kind of became our theme tune for the Six Nations and would be put straight on in the changing rooms after each game.

At that point, people were saying it was a good start to the championship and perhaps we could do a Triple Crown, but that there was no way we were going to beat France in Paris.

I don't think it's an overstatement to say that's a match that changed my life. Yet while everyone remembers the two tries I scored in quick succession after half-time, the thing that sticks in my mind is how well Stephen Jones played that day. In the second half, he just ran the show for us.

Mind you, in the first half, it was the French who ran the show. They seemed to have all the ball and they were carving us up left, right and centre. I remember we were behind the posts after they scored one of their tries and it just felt as though it could be a long, long day. But somehow we managed to hang on in there with some last-ditch defence and then Stephen landed a penalty just before half-time to make it 15–6, which was nowhere near a reflection on the half. We could easily have been thirty or thirty-five points down.

I've lost track of the number of people who've asked me what was said in our dressing room at half-time. There's a myth that some Churchill-like speech was made by somebody.

The truth is that hardly anything was said. There was no great speech by anyone or a 'let's do it for the country' message. I wish there had been, because it would have made for a much better story! But, to be honest, it was fairly calm and quite laid back, just quite normal really. Nothing sticks in my head about that half-time at all.

I wouldn't say we changed our gameplan for the second half, but we just went out with the attitude that we had nothing to lose and that's when you sometimes play your best rugby.

We had been totally outplayed and we'd lost our skipper, with Gareth 'Alfie' Thomas breaking his thumb, so it was a case of 'let's just play'. And that's what we did.

It was Stephen who set the ball rolling by shocking everyone with a 60-metre break. I don't think he'd ever gone so far, so fast, in his life!

I had come up from a ruck and, instead of following the ball, I stayed wide, which is something Scott Johnson always stressed to us. He'd say: 'Don't all follow the ball, keep your width.' That's what I did and it paid off. When the ball eventually came to me in the centre position, I knew Shane Williams was outside me and I just thought I had to get the ball to him as quickly as I could, so he could do something. I gave the pass straight away and followed him on his inside shoulder because, nine times out of ten, he'll get the ball away. Shane had had a tough time with his opposite number Aurelien Rougerie in the first half, but this was his revenge, as he skinned Rougerie and gave the scoring pass back to me on the inside.

Suddenly it was a different game and, within a couple of minutes, we were on the attack again in their twenty-two. Michael Owen had just got held up short from a tap penalty when we were awarded another one. I don't know why, but I decided to tap and go for the line. If I saw someone else do it I would be screaming at them. You've got a penalty 5 metres out, you either go for goal or kick to the corner. But I found the ball in my hands and I thought I'm going for it. It was just pure instinct.

The French skipper Fabien Pelous was in front of me, but I kind of half side-stepped him, reached out and just managed to get over. The first thing I remember thinking was, 'I can't believe I just did that,' and the second thing was I was gutted we had another half hour to hold on. I just wanted the game to finish there and then, because I knew they were going to come back at us.

Looking back at that try, it makes you realise what a fine line there is between being the hero and the villain. If I hadn't scored, everyone would have been having a go at me. Luckily for me I just crept over and everyone now says what a good decision it was. Such are the narrow margins between success and failure, especially at international level. Careers can hinge on little things like that.

The last five to ten minutes of that game in Paris were probably the longest of my life, because they threw absolutely everything at us. But the way we refused to crack just summed up how close we had become as a group. We had four or five scrums on our line, where the front row held out, and where we displayed some incredible scrambling defence.

When Stephen kicked the ball out and the final whistle went to signal a 24–18 victory, it was an amazing feeling. There were loads of Welsh fans in that corner doing their nut and all the boys were just going crazy. Although beating England had been a big win, this was even bigger,

*Top*: With my beautiful wife Sam on our wedding day in September 2005. She was amazing in organising the entire event in just two weeks. It meant so much to us that my mum Julie was able to attend. Here we are with my stepdad Paul.

*Centre left*: Five generations: Great grandmother Nancy, grandmother Val, mum Julie, me and Mia.

*Centre right*: Holding Mia, a few hours after she was born, January 2003.

Rugby matters, but my family matters most.

*Bottom left*: Mia's first day at school.

*Bottom right*: That's my boy: Corey a few months old.

*Top*: The day I realised my childhood ambition of winning my first Wales cap, against the Barbarians in August 1996. We beat them 31–10, too!

*Bottom*: This game against Canada in August 1999 was one of the first international fixtures to be played in the new Millennium Stadium in Cardiff. This was a good time for the national team and we felt we could go far in the forthcoming World Cup.

© Huw Evans

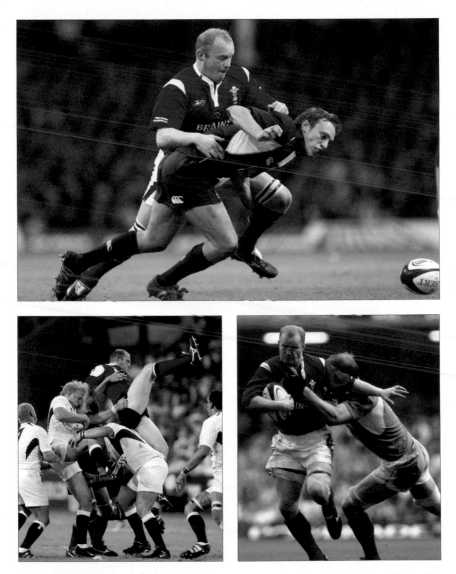

Playing for Wales is an honour. Rugby means so much to the Welsh public and every time I run onto the pitch I know I have the expectations of my country to fulfil.

*Top*: Beating Scotland in February 2006.

*Bottom left*: At the World Cup in Australia in 2005. I came on as a replacement to score a try against England.

*Bottom right*: In action against Ireland during the Grand Slam-clinching victory in March 2005.

© *Huw Evans*

*Top*: New Zealand is an awesome rugby-playing nation. The All Blacks are such an efficient fighting force, and I've been on the receiving end of some of the toughest rugbymen in the world, including the legendary Jonah Lomu.

*Bottom*: Australia are a formidable force too, but on this occasion at the Millennium stadium, in November 2005, we beat them 24-22.

*Top*: It was no easy feat, but winning the Grand Slam of the 2005 Six Nations and being crowned player of the championship was a career high. Here I am taking on Ireland's Paul O'Connor during our 32–30 win.

*Bottom left*: The following year's campaign was even tougher, and the French proved too good for us. I'm pictured tackling Florian Fritz just before his try puts France into the lead.

*Bottom right*: Jonny Wilkinson is a world-class fly-half and was too quick for to catch during this match.

© *Huw*

*Top left*: Taking the lineout ball for Wales. Being able to rely 100 per cent on your team mates and working together for a good result (*top right*) is one of the best feelings in the world.

*Bottom left*: You have to strike the right balance between taking the job seriously and being able to have a laugh. At the training camp with Gareth Thomas and the lads, January 2007.

*Bottom right*: At the end of the day it's about getting the right results, and taking time to thank the fans for their support is so important. Arriving back in Cardiff after our victory in Paris, February 2005.

© *Huw Evans*

*Top*: With some of my predecessors, Welsh rugby captains from over the past 40 years.

© *Huw Evans*

*Bottom left*: I am always so proud to represent Wales on the pitch.

*Bottom right*: Even though our departure from the 2007 World Cup in France was earlier than we would have liked, we had a couple of fantastic matches. Here I am during our 42–17 drubbing of Canada at the Stade de la Beaujoire in Nantes.

© *Clevar*

Beating France to win my second Gland Slam in 2008 was a pretty clear sign that coming out of retirement had been the right decision.

*Top*: To score the try that sealed the Slam was just the icing on the cake.

*Bottom*: Celebrating with Jon Thomas and Ryan Jones, the back row boys.

© *Huw Evans*

coming away from home – and it was such a great game and such a great comeback.

I remember ringing my mother up straight after the game to speak to her. She had been diagnosed with cancer in the January, so it was quite an emotional moment. She was never one to go over the top about how well a game had gone or how well I'd played, but she said she'd had a few friends over and everyone was going crazy back home.

The boys had a good night in Paris after that, but I actually had quite a low-key evening. Alfie couldn't drink because of the painkillers for his thumb, so Michael Owen and I, along with a couple of the management, stayed with him at our hotel. We were in a great spot, right on the Champs Elysees, and we just had a few drinks there and reflected on what we'd achieved that day. A few of the other boys probably wished they'd stayed in too, seeing the state of them the next morning. There's a famous photo of Tom Shanklin looking like a ghost!

But I don't think anybody begrudged the boys going out and celebrating that one, because it had been one of the greatest Welsh comebacks in living memory and a result that had been so unexpected. At times like that you've just got to enjoy the moment, because you never knew when a win like that is going to happen again. As I say, it's a game that probably changed my life and I did get recognised a lot more after that.

On the Monday there was a picture of me giving a two-fingered victory salute on the front page of the *Daily Telegraph*, not the sports section but the front of the paper itself. I remember my best mate Jamie's wife

Lindsay texting me after that and saying, 'You've really made it now, you are on the front of the *Telegraph*!' That's when what I'd done, and what we'd done as a team, started to sink in.

It was when we got back that all the hype really started. The attention we got after that win was amazing and we didn't really know what we were doing for a while.

Although I had been playing for Wales for eight or nine years by then, that's when I really realised just how much the sport means to the Welsh public and how much they'd been dying for success.

Next up was Scotland in Murrayfield and I just remember in the week leading up to that game how intense the media coverage seemed to be and how much press work there was to do. I did a lot of one-on-one interviews, which I hadn't done so much of before, and I found myself in demand. They even did a little profile on me for *Grandstand*, to go out on the day of the game, which again was something that had never happened before.

It did go to another level during that period and we could see how much of an effect we were having on the nation and how people were getting caught up in it all. Everyone was saying we were going to blow Scotland away and people were already talking about a Grand Slam decider against Ireland the following week.

But the management did a really good job in keeping our feet on the ground. I remember Alun Carter, our analyst, saying: 'Put your hands up if you've won in Murrayfield,' and I think Gareth Llewellyn was the only one. I'd drawn up there, so I wasn't sure whether or not to half raise my arm! But it just hammered home to us how difficult it is to go there and win.

It seemed as though the whole world was watching us going into that Scotland game and it also seemed as though half of Wales was following us to Edinburgh. You always see a lot of red in the airport when you're flying out from Cardiff for an international and it's usually pretty lively for the Scotland and Ireland games because you get a different clientele to the Paris and Rome trips. But this time you could sense something was different, because there were so many fans there. Yet not even that could prepare us for Murrayfield.

When we ran out to warm up before the game, we couldn't believe our eyes. It was just a sea of red. It's usually quite empty at that stage, an hour or so before kick-off, but everyone had got in there really early and all you could see was red. You can't underestimate how much of a lift that gave the boys. It felt like a home game.

I don't know if it was because of that or because we were so confident at the time, but that first half was the best half of rugby I've ever been part of. From the word go everything came off. I remember Shanks showboating and flicking the ball behind his back; I did a reverse pass at scrum-half; and you even had the front-five forwards joining in with the tricks. It wasn't that we were being arrogant; it's just that we were enjoying our rugby so much and had the confidence to try things.

I think the ball-in-play time set a new record for the championship and it's certainly one of the quickest games I've ever played in. Incredibly, we were 38–3 up at half-time and we kind of took our foot off the gas. It was like this game's won, let's get it over with and prepare for next week because we've got a Grand Slam decider coming up. Still, a 46–22 scoreline was convincing enough.

There was only a six-day turnaround ahead of the final game against Ireland, but the management handled us brilliantly. We did little physical work that week and they kept us all together at the team hotel. You knew what was going on outside, you only had to turn the news on to see how big it was, but the management kept us away from all that and kept us really tight as a group. That was definitely a good move. This was the biggest match of our careers and we didn't want anything to distract us from the job in hand.

It was probably also a good thing that it was only a six-day turnaround. If it had been longer, we might have started thinking about the game too much. As it was, we had such little time to get sucked in by it all.

We might not have seen much of the public during the course of the week, but that all changed on the day of the match.

Normally on the drive into Cardiff for a game, you see the odd Welsh jersey along the way. But this time was different. Wherever you looked, the place was just ram-packed with people decked out in red. And when we actually got close to the stadium, it was crazy. I'd never seen anything like it before, and I'd had fifty-odd caps by then. The reaction of the supporters when they saw the team bus and the noise they made just made the hairs on the back of your neck stand up.

I have to admit that's as nervous as I've ever been going into a game and I know a lot of the other boys felt the same. But, as a group, it was a case of saying, 'Let's not get involved in all the emotion. Let's keep calm and concentrate on the gameplan.' Thankfully, we managed to do just that.

Mind you, I don't know if we'd have been able to handle the pressure as well if we'd seen how many thousands of people were outside City Hall waiting to watch the game on a big screen. We knew it was a big occasion that day, but we had no idea just how big it had become. When we saw those pictures of the scenes at City Hall the next day, we couldn't believe it.

It wasn't until after the game that we saw any of the things that had been going on, like Max Boyce singing out on the pitch and getting the crowd going, but it was probably just as well, because we were nervous enough as it was. We just wanted to get out and play, which is what we did.

As it turned out, you couldn't have scripted the day better. It was so nice outside and the game went like a dream. Gethin Jenkins' charge-down try was a big moment, because it meant we were in front and could relax and start playing. Gavin Henson landed a drop goal and a huge penalty as we built our lead and then Kevin Morgan scored the killer try. While most of the boys mobbed Kev, I went straight to Tom Shanklin, who had set up the score with a superb break. I just said, 'That was world class, mate.' Shanks was immense in the centre against Brian O'Driscoll that day. When you play Ireland, if you don't stop O'Driscoll they'll probably beat you. But Shanks just dominated him that day.

Taking nothing away from Dwayne Peel, who also had

a great game, but how Tom didn't pick up the Man of the Match award that day I'll never know.

Kev's try meant we were well in front, but there was still plenty of time left and every one of us was guilty of clock-watching, which is the very thing we'd spoken about not doing. But even though Ireland came back with a couple of tries, there was no catching us. And come the final play, with us well clear at 32–20, it was left to me to end the game. The ball spilled out in front of me and I just couldn't wait to get it off the park. Then came the final whistle and everyone started going nuts. But I didn't jump up because, as I kicked the ball off, O'Driscoll was right in front of me and the first thing I did was to shake his hand. He was great about it all and just said, 'Well done, you boys deserve it.'

We stayed on the pitch for ages afterwards, doing a lap of honour after receiving the championship trophy, and it was just great to soak up the atmosphere. We'd worked so hard for this moment and you just wanted to savour it and take it all in.

I was handed the trophy at one point to pose for the photographers and I just remember grabbing Kevin to be in the shot with me. That photo of us two holding the cup is now synonymous with that day. It's been everywhere and it's quite fitting because we were Pontypridd youth boys together and we'd shared in some tough times for Wales over the years.

When we finally got back into the dressing room, we changed into our tuxedos for the after-match function and it was then I was told I'd been voted player of the tournament by the public, which was a massive honour. I was given the trophy again and a bottle of champagne to pose for some more pictures and one of those takes pride of place in our dining room at home. To be recognised by the public with an award like that means a hell of a lot.

Before we left the stadium, we went back out onto the pitch in our tuxes for a big team photo and then it was onto the bus for the ride over to the Hilton Hotel for the post-match dinner. That's hardly any distance at all, but it seemed to take us forever, with the streets just teaming with people celebrating Wales' first Grand Slam since 1978.

That bus ride to the Hilton was crazy. It's the closest we'll ever be to being pop stars. We couldn't get off the bus because there were so many people outside the hotel. We had to go in through the workman's entrance, via the back door and through the kitchens. It's the kind of thing you see in the films with pop stars. Even though it was the back entrance, we were still struggling to get in there and the police and security had to make a gateway for us and our wives. I don't think I'm over-exaggerating when I say it was that mental that night.

After the dinner, we went on to a private function, which Brains brewers had arranged at their base. That was really nice for the boys. No one else was allowed in there, just the players and their families.

We eventually got back to the Vale at about midnight and that's when it got a little bit blurry! All I can remember is being with my wife and Dwayne Peel and his girlfriend. There was an Irish band playing in the hotel bar and it was ram packed in there. Then our coach, Mike Ruddock, brought his guitar out and started doing a few numbers. Don't ask me what time I got to bed, but let's just say I didn't get much sleep that night.

The next day, Brains put on a function at The Yard pub in town and we all met up at about 2pm in the afternoon. That was a long day and by about 9pm I just remember thinking I wanted to go home, which I did. I was one very tired, but also very happy man. It had been the end of an amazing journey.

# chapter 15

# shunned by sir clive

The 2005 British Lions tour of New Zealand should have been the pinnacle of my career. Instead, it's a trip I look back on with feelings of frustration and bitterness.

There had never been a Lions tour like it before in terms of the size of the party or the hype leading up to us leaving these shores. It seemed that hype had been going on for months and months, with the appointment of Sir Clive Woodward as coach having heightened media interest in the trip.

Woodward had guided England to World Cup glory in 2003, giving rugby the kind of profile it had never had before in the UK, and now he was aiming to achieve similar success with the Lions. Wherever Woodward went in the 2004–05 season the media followed and the question was always which player was he watching now.

During the November internationals, he came to spend a week with the Welsh camp, in an observational role, which inevitably led to a fair bit of banter among the boys. It was a running joke that if anyone spoke to him or trained too well in front of him that they'd get stick from the other boys. It would be 'Oh Clive's about is he?' There was a load of mickey taking with people accusing each other of trying to get themselves on the Lions tour.

In truth, we didn't really have that much to do with him that week. I bumped into him once in the team hotel and said a brief hello and that was it. The next time I was to meet him was some six months later – after he'd chosen me to be one of his Lions.

A lot had happened by then, with Wales doing the clean sweep in the Six Nations and me being named player of the tournament. To be honest, I would have been disappointed not to be selected after the championship I'd had, but it was still a special moment to hear my name announced as part of the squad. You don't have a letter or a phone call the night before to say you are in, you just hear the same as everyone else, and I heard it on the radio in the physio room in Cardiff.

But there wasn't such good news for all my Grand Slam team-mates, with the likes of Kevin Morgan, Brent Cockbain and Mefin Davies missing out, which caused something of an outcry. It was a complete reversal of 2001 really. Back then people had said there were too many Welshmen on the trip; now they were saying there weren't enough.

While disappointed for those boys who had been

overlooked, I was obviously delighted to be in and was looking forward to getting started. I couldn't have dreamed of a better Six Nations and now I was out to carry that form onto the Lions. Whereas in 2001 I'd just been happy to be part of the squad, this time I was aiming for a Test place.

Before leaving for New Zealand, we all met at the Vale of Glamorgan Hotel, which had been chosen as the pre-tour base. From day one, the first thing you noticed was just how efficiently things were run under Woodward's regime.

There's a big function room upstairs at the Vale hotel which we use for team meetings when we are in camp with Wales. There's usually a couple of tables and some chairs and that's about it. But when we arrived there for our first Lions meeting, it was just a bit different. You walked in and there were giant plasma screens, music blaring out of a sound system and a podium with a microphone. We were thinking we must have stumbled into a press conference by mistake, but there was no press there, it was just the boys.

In team meetings, you usually just sit by whoever, but this time all your names were on the tables with places to sit. Clive got up first and introduced his back-room team, which took a while in itself because there so many of them, and then a player from each nation got up to speak. There was Ireland's Brian O'Driscoll, the tour captain, England's Martin Corry, Scotland's Gordon Bulloch and our own Gareth 'Alfie' Thomas. They had all obviously been prepped beforehand and in turn they said what the players from their respective countries would bring to the tour. We were all given these big red folders embroidered with our names on them and were left thinking to ourselves, 'How much work has gone into all this?' It was all very impressive and it felt important.

That was the first impression you got of Clive, how efficient he was and how much detail he'd gone into just for that week. Everything was there for us and every possible scenario seemed to have been planned for. As well as a host of coaches, we also had our own chef and solicitor, while Alastair Campbell, the former Downing Street 'spin doctor', had been drafted in to help out with the media side of things. We were looked after like nothing I have experienced before. So it boded well.

Not that everything about that week was really my cup of tea. I have to admit that I wasn't particularly keen on some of the team-building exercises. I enjoyed the outdoor ones we did in 2001, where we were climbing things and going on assault courses. But this time it was all indoors and one of the things we had to do was paint this collage. We all had to paint different segments and when you put them together it made up a Lions motif. I wasn't a big fan of that, but I got on with it and didn't say anything – unlike Gavin Henson.

Speaking to a reporter afterwards, he admitted he hadn't thought much of the exercises and his comments were picked up everywhere. He got a fair bit of stick for what he said. I remember all the English guys saying, 'Clive won't be happy with that.' And he probably wasn't. He'd put so much store and effort into all of this and one of the biggest names in the squad was saying he didn't know what was going on. But Gav was just being honest and saying he didn't get a lot out of it.

A lot of it is difficult to take on board and it's case of each to their own, but you can see why they want to do it. You've got a short space of time for everyone to get to know each other. You've got to break the ice as quickly as possible and that's the way a lot of coaches look to do it.

Perhaps I'm a bit old school, but I think there are simpler ways of getting to know each other. The best bonding session we had during that week was when a group of us went out for the night in Cardiff. The boys who weren't playing in the warm-up game against Argentina were told to go out on the Saturday night, so myself, Tom Shanklin and Dwayne Peel took O'Driscoll, Matt Dawson, Paul O'Connell and a few others into Cardiff for the evening. That was one of the best nights we had during our time together as Lions.

There had been a lot of attention on us during that week in Wales, but from the moment we landed in New Zealand it all moved up to a totally different level. It felt as though every single pair of eyes in the country were on us and we were really under the microscope. They may say Wales is intense for rugby, but it's got absolutely nothing on New Zealand.

With the way the tour was being built up, with Sir Clive in charge, all the coaches and backroom staff we had and with this big PR machine headed by Campbell, the Kiwis were licking their lips and saying they couldn't wait to get into us.

In fairness to Campbell, he was a really interesting guy to speak to because he was such a knowledgeable bloke. He's been there and done it and knows a lot of stuff, so he was great to speak to. But it probably just added fuel to the fire for the Kiwis with him being there; his presence added to the over-the-top feeling that was starting to grow.

Our opening game was against the Bay of Plenty, which is somewhere most people in this country have probably never heard of. But from that very first match, we had a huge wake-up call about how tough the tour was going to be. We won 34–20, but it was hard work and we knew there were far stiffer challenges ahead.

Even though I was selected for that game, I just had a feeling from the outset that things were stacked against me getting into the Test team. I just felt the whole set-up on tour was heavily based around the English system. You had Woodward, Andy Robinson and Phil Larder, you had the fitness guy, Dave Reddin, you had the manager, you even had the chef. Although you had coaches from the other nations there, they were basically with the Wednesday team. When it came to the Saturday team, there was a huge English influence.

And I could just sense from day one that they were going to go with the old guard. They were going to go with the tried and tested, with the people that had won them the World Cup. The plan was to replicate that success using the same formula.

You could see where they were coming from to an extent because what England did in 2003 was obviously brilliant and those guys knew what to do to win huge Test matches. But those players were also two years older and things had moved on. But that was ignored. When it came to selection, especially for the first Test, Woodward was to pick on 2003 form rather than 2005 form. You didn't need to be a rocket scientist to see that.

Any hopes I had of persuading him otherwise went up in smoke with the game against the New Zealand Maoris. It had been built up as the fourth Test and we got mullered. We were taken apart up front that night and given a total lesson. They took our scrum away, they took our line-out away and they battered us in the contact area. I was up against Marty Holah, who turned over loads of ball and was named man of the match. Our pack was blamed for that 19–13 defeat and I found myself on the receiving end of a lot of stick. But nobody from the management came and said to me: 'You could have done this or done that.' It was as if I was kind of hung out to dry after that game.

Neil Back came in for the Wellington game the following Wednesday and they won that well – and that was goodbye to my chances of starting the first Test. It was the same for Michael Owen as well, but whichever back-row boys played in that Maoris game would have suffered exactly the same fate.

It's a big bugbear of mine when people go on about the breakdown area and point the finger, because it's what leads up to the breakdown that counts. That's why the New Zealanders are so much better than us in that department. We are still struggling in the contact area compared to them now, but two years ago we were nowhere near their level. We just weren't used to that level of intensity. That Maoris game was a real lesson on how hard New Zealand rugby is.

During the de-brief afterwards I just felt there was no real plan from the coaches of how we were going to fix the problem, which was disappointing. To me that suggested they didn't know what to do. Instead of looking to rectify the problems we'd encountered, we were basically dispensed with. They didn't cure the problem, they just got rid of it. That's when I started getting frustrated with the tour and I didn't really enjoy myself from that point on.

You are never confident of your place when you are on tour with the likes of Back, Richard Hill and Lewis Moody. You know it's going to be a fight for the jersey but, given the way things had gone in the Six Nations, I had thought I would be in with a shout of starting the first Test.

But the English press were behind their men and Back got in ahead of me, while Jonny Wilkinson was chosen ahead of Gavin Henson in the centre. Now Jonny and Back have done everything there is in the game and they are world-class players, but you can't deny that at the time a lot of those English guys got picked on reputation rather than form. It was a case of bring in the old boys, while the likes of myself were just brushed to one side. The first Test showed just how much of a mistake that policy was.

A lot of us Welsh boys felt hard done by and we were all frustrated with the gameplan. We knew we weren't going to beat New Zealand the way the coaches wanted to play. The autumn before we had lost by just a point to them by moving the ball about and we felt that's what the

Lions had to do as well. I felt we had to play to our strengths and that would have suited a lot of the other players out there as well.

But the coaches had a preconceived idea that they were going to go down to New Zealand and batter their front five, which was ridiculous. They were saying they were weak there. They weren't weak anywhere.

It was difficult because everyone was playing a different style. The Welsh boys weren't used to the way the English were used to playing and vice versa. With such a short space of time together, it's difficult to gel such different approaches.

The Welsh boys were caught between a rock and a hard place. We wanted to play like Wales did, but the coaches who coached Wales weren't with us. It got to the point where we weren't exactly sure how we wanted to play it.

Having come unstuck in the first Test in Christchurch, losing 21–3, the coaches then tried to change course midstream and made a load of changes, but the damage had already been done.

We went on to lose the series 3–0 and there were precious few positives to take out of the trip, but one of the few was the emergence of Alfie as a great Lions leader.

Everyone was devastated after the first Test, not just because of the result but because our skipper O'Driscoll was out of the tour after damaging his shoulder in the opening couple of minutes.

We went back to the hotel and there was a lot of talk about who the captain would be now. We just all assumed it would be Martin Corry, because he had taken over in the first Test, so it was a big shock when Alfie was appointed.

He had come out late because of his club commitments with Toulouse and when he arrived Clive had pulled him to one side for a chat. Alfie was just really straight with him and said how he felt we should be playing. I think Clive was taken aback by that and it made a big impression.

When Alfie told me that Clive had asked him to be captain for the second Test in Wellington, I said: 'You're taking the mick.' Alfie can't be Lions captain. That was my first thought. I was shocked like he was, but all the boys bought into him straight away.

He was totally different to O'Driscoll. He's a lot more laid back and more of a joker than any other captain would be and that was exactly what we needed.

The way he acts you don't really associate with a Lions captain. He's a bag of fun all the time. He spoke to Tony Blair on the phone and it was: 'How are you butt?' That's just how Alfie is. He didn't put on airs or graces just because he became Lions captain or because he was speaking to someone famous. He just said what he thought.

For the Welsh boys it was brilliant, because we knew what he was like, but the boys from the other countries bought into it as well and enjoyed playing under him. He just puts a smile on people's faces, yet when it's rugby time he's as switched on as anyone.

While Alfie came out of the tour with his reputation enhanced, Woodward ended up taking a hell of a lot of stick. He didn't really get involved with the coaching, he just oversaw everything and made sure we were prepared off the field. On that front you couldn't fault him. We had our own plane chartered everywhere, we stayed in the best hotels, we had our own rooms and the best food. Everything was spot on, apart from what we were really there for – the rugby.

In all fairness, the Kiwis were just too good for us. I felt that in the provincial games as well, and the Tests just hammered it home, with the style of rugby they were playing and how intelligent they all were at doing their jobs. They were just streets ahead of us. But we didn't help our cause. Some people have said there were too many players on the trip. I don't know if that was the case, but we definitely had too many people off the field. The whole thing had just become too big and too much like a military operation.

The one thing that kept me sane was being with the Midweek Massive, the name we gave to the midweek side. It was much more relaxed in that environment, with Ian McGeechan and Gareth Jenkins in charge. We really enjoyed it and were unbeaten, winning five out of five, culminating in a 17–13 victory over Auckland at Eden Park, where I scored my one try on the trip. Training and things were a lot more relaxed with the 'Massive' and how I felt a Lions side should be run, whereas I felt it was a little bit too regimented with Andy Robinson and Eddie O'Sullivan in the Saturday side.

I was part of that first-team set-up for the second and third Tests in Wellington and Auckland, where I sat on the bench, but that proved the most galling experience of the whole trip.

Having been a replacement in all three Tests in Australia in 2001 without getting on the field, it now looked as though history was going to repeat itself. I watched on from the sidelines for eighty minutes in Wellington as we lost 48–18 and it seemed I was going to miss out yet again in Auckland.

I can remember sitting there in the third Test at Eden Park: we were getting a hammering and everyone was going on apart from me. Alfie was just laughing at me and saying: 'You are not going to go on again.' I had to laugh at myself because I was nearly crying. There were ten minutes to go and I was just saying to myself: 'Put me on. We are not going to win. I'm not going to lose it for you, don't worry.'

Then, eventually, with about four minutes left, I had the call to get on there. I got my hands on the ball once I think. So that's two Lions tours, five Tests on the bench and a grand total of four minutes on the field!

I'm not bitter about much during my career, but I am bitter about that 2005 tour. In 2001, in Australia, I just went there in hope. I probably didn't feel I was ready for the Tests but, four years later, I felt I was worthy of a place and could handle my own. It was a lot more frustrating.

I've got huge respect for Neil Back and when he was at his peak he was an awesome player, but he was thirty-six and hadn't played international rugby for two years, and I just feel I should have been the one to get the chance in the first test given what I had achieved that season.

After that, Lewis Moody got the nod at seven for the next two Tests and I've got no qualms over that, because he played superbly out there. But that first Test will always rankle with me.

The great irony was that it was supposed to be the tour the players would enjoy after the whingeing of 2001. Yet, when push comes to shove, I can honestly say I enjoyed that trip to Australia far more.

## chapter 16

# brought to book

I've never really seen myself as someone who's courted controversy, so it came as something of a shock to find myself caught up in one a couple of years ago.

It was the autumn of 2005 and it all centred around the book that my high-profile Wales team-mate Gavin Henson had brought out. I'd heard that he was doing an autobiography, but I hadn't really given it much thought and I certainly didn't expect to figure in it to any great extent. So I was in for a bit of a surprise.

The first I knew of it was when somebody said to me: 'What do you think about what Gav has written about you?' and I just said: 'What are you on about?'

Anyway, I managed to get hold of a copy of the book and, after a bit of searching, I found the bit about me. It centred around a Celtic League match between the Cardiff Blues and the Ospreys at the Arms Park on New Year's Day 2005. What Gavin had done was to write about an incident between the two of us during that game.

209

He described how I had come flying in and started throwing punches at him and how I was screaming: 'You don't like it in the face, do you, pretty boy! You can't handle it.'

When I read it, I was a bit surprised to see that in there. But I couldn't really have any complaints about it, because all of it was true!

What I remember of the incident is that Gav had put a hell of a hit in on our scrum-half Ryan Powell and he was whooping and giving it loads. I thought to myself, 'Who is this Flash Harry? Who does he think he is?' and I kind of lost it with him. It was a real nip-and-tuck game and emotions were running high, as they often do in Welsh derbies, and I guess I got caught up in the moment.

After the game, I apologised to him and admitted it was my fault and I didn't think anything more of it for the next nine months or so – until it appeared in his book.

I was a bit surprised, because I didn't think it had been that big an incident. It was neither a big deal to me nor was it big news, because that kind of banter happens in every game.

When I saw Gav next I spoke to him about it and he didn't apologise, he just explained that he put it in there because he wanted to show how competitive the game is and what happens out on the field.

If he'd lied about it in the book, I wouldn't have been happy, but it was accurate. It actually happened and I did say what he said I did, so I haven't really got that much argument with it and we laugh about it now.

But, at the time, his book created a hell of a stink. It

wasn't just me he'd written about, but a lot of other players, both from opposing teams and within the Welsh squad, and some of the things he'd said were pretty controversial.

He'd questioned the residency rule that allowed the likes of Brent Cockbain, Sonny Parker and Hal Luscombe to play for Wales and he hadn't been too flattering about Garan Evans, the Llanelli player who had gone to the 2003 World Cup ahead of him. He'd also accused the Ireland captain Brian O'Driscoll of trying to gouge him in the eye during the 2005 Grand Slam game in Cardiff, which didn't go down well with O'Driscoll at all.

I think there were a lot of people who didn't like the fact that Gav had done a book when he was so young. If he'd been at the end of his career, it might have been a different story.

As I say, I wasn't really bothered over what he'd written about me, because it was true, but there was a feeling within the Welsh squad that maybe he'd overstepped the mark a bit with some of the things he'd written.

Our skipper, Gareth 'Alfie' Thomas, certainly felt that way. To Alfie, the fact that we were so tight and so close as a group was really important. He felt what Gav had done wasn't in the best interests of the squad. I think he felt Gav was too inexperienced and too young to express those feelings publicly at the time.

As a group, we wanted to deal with it internally and we felt we had to set a precedent in case anybody else was thinking about going out and slagging anyone off.

So Gav, who was out injured at the time, was asked to

come in and meet the rest of the squad to discuss it, which he did, and he ended up apologising if he'd upset anyone. A lot has been made of that, but it wasn't really a massive deal. It was just in the team room before a meeting.

As far as we were concerned, that was the end of the matter. We all thought it had been put to bed. But we were wrong.

It all blew up again, with dramatic consequences, following the game against England at the start of the 2006 Six Nations. Gavin wasn't playing in that match because he was suspended, but he still ended up being the centre of attention.

I'm not really one to read the match programme and I hadn't looked at it for that England game at Twickenham. But after that game, a couple of the boys said: 'Did you read the article about Gavin?' So I took a look.

What had happened was that the journalist who had ghost-written Gav's book, Graham Thomas of BBC Wales, had done an article in the programme. In it, he said he felt Gavin had been unfairly treated and that he had nothing to apologise for. That upset most of the boys because we thought the whole episode was over and done with and here it was rearing its head again. It was as if Graham was sticking two fingers up to the boys and saying: 'Who are you to tell me what to do?'

As far as we were concerned, we were just trying to keep true to the values and ethics we had created in our squad, values we felt had moved us on over the course of the previous four years. A lot of us had worked really hard from the dark days when we lost ten in a row. We'd been through all the flak and, if anything, the team spirit is what had made us. Once things like Gav's book start coming out, that's what we felt was going to break us. As soon as one person starts doing it, then everyone will and we felt it was important to nip it in the bud. It was a case of trying to protect something we cared about. It wasn't that big a deal with Gavin, but Graham made it a big deal by coming out with that article.

The boys wanted to make a stand, because, as I say, we felt he had just stuck his two fingers up to us. So we said for the build-up to the next game against Scotland that we didn't want Graham in there at the press conferences. We wanted to make our feelings known to him. Although he had the power to write that article, we wanted to have the power to show him we were upset with what he'd done. That was the general feeling and it was made clear that he wasn't to be there.

But somehow the message didn't get through. Whether it was because of a breakdown in communication or whatever, I don't know, but when we went to the main press session that week at Glamorgan County Cricket Club in Sophia Gardens, he was there.

As soon as Alfie saw him, he just walked straight out of the room where the main press conference with the captain and coach was due to be held. We were all in another room waiting to do our interviews and the first we knew of what had happened was when our press officer Simon Rimmer came in and told us. It was panic stations then. I remember Simon coming up to me and saying: 'You've got to go in there, you've got to go in there.'

We asked him to give us five minutes and we spoke as

a group. We just felt that if we went in there, it was going to look bad on Alfie, as if he was the only one boycotting it, so we came to a group decision of one-out, all-out. We couldn't be seen to go against him. So we stayed put.

Alfie wasn't there at this point. He had gone. He had made his point and left. After him, I was probably the most senior player, so I ended up getting a call on my mobile from Alan Phillips, the team manager, who was somewhere else at the time. He'd obviously been told what had happened and he came on and said: 'Mart, you've got to get them in there.'

But I explained the situation to him and I think he could see our side of the story, that if we went in there, Alfie was going to be hung out to dry. We felt it was better for all fifteen of us to take a bit of stick rather than just for all of it to land on Alfie. And fair play to the younger players, they went along with it. That they were to ready to back their skipper too, just showed how tight we were. We wanted to make a point. It was the first time as a team we'd done that, but we all felt it was the right thing to do.

All this time, our coach Mike Ruddock had been on his own dealing with the media, trying to handle questions about what was going on and why the players weren't there. He had spoken to Michael Owen, who had been captain before, and asked him to join him at the main press conference in Alfie's place. It was a Catch 22 situation for Michael because he didn't want to upset the head coach, but he didn't want to upset all the boys either. So he said he couldn't do it.

In fact, there was only one Welsh player in there with the media while the boycott was going on, Mark Jones, the Scarlets winger. He had been late turning up and had gone straight past the room where we all were and into the one where the press were waiting. So he was there getting interviewed, happy as Larry, not having a clue what was going on down the corridor. He's still bagging it to this day over that.

But that was the only funny part of the whole episode. Graham had stood his ground and refused to leave, which is understandable, so there was a real impasse and it seemed to go on for a long time. Eventually, we saw Graham sloping out and we did go in there. But, by then, our no-show had become *the* story for the press.

You knew it was going to be a big deal, but we were willing to take the flak. To some people what we did might seem childish but, as players, it's sometimes difficult to have your say. We wanted to make our point that you can't do the kind of thing Graham did without us being entitled to have our say back.

Some people have said the fact that we refused to follow Mike into the press conference was evidence of him having lost his authority over us. And that theory gained popularity when he resigned the following week and people started claiming he'd been forced out by player-power. But when we took that stand at the press conference, it was nothing against Mike. It was just an issue between the players and one journalist.

Of course, the fact that it also involved Gavin made it all the more of a story for the press. The guy has got a bigger profile than anyone else in the game today, with his relationship with his pop star girlfriend Charlotte Church meaning he's on the front pages as often as he is on the back pages.

People often ask how we dealt with that within the Welsh squad. If it was any other group of players, we might have struggled with it. But there's good humour within the squad and he's just one of the boys. He doesn't get treated any differently and there's no jealousy. There's plenty of mickey taking mind you, especially when you see him on the Jonathan Ross show and things like that. He gets a lot of stick off the lads, but he takes it well and he does take the mick out of himself really well.

Sometimes I do feel a bit sorry for him, because he's got the paparazzi on his tail the whole time. He can't go anywhere without a camera being thrust in his face. Earlier last year, there were pictures of him and Charlotte visiting a French ski resort plastered all over the papers. I could have gone skiing at the same time and nobody would have cared, but because Gav has got a celebrity girlfriend, a huge issue is made of it. He's probably just doing things that normal people are doing, but it gets blown out of all proportion.

We got our first taste of his new lifestyle on the night of the Grand Slam-clinching victory over Ireland in March 2005. He had just started seeing Charlotte and there were deals going on left, right and centre about who would have the first picture of the two of them that night. With him and Charlotte and the Grand Slam, it all just came together at once and his profile was right up there. We were at a function put on by Brains brewers that night and the two of them ended up being escorted out a different way from everyone else to try and avoid the photographers.

The following day, Brains put on a private party for us at a bar called The Yard in the centre of Cardiff and Gav probably had a little bit too much too drink and things got a bit out of hand. That kind of thing happens all the time but, because of who he was, a massive thing was made of it. That's the difficulty for him all the time.

When he first came into the Wales squad, around 2001, he was very quiet, and not comfortable at speaking in front of a group. I remember one day he was supposed to give a presentation to the players and instead of doing it he went home! I think that's understandable, because a lot of people aren't comfortable doing things like that, especially when they are young.

But I think he has come out of his shell a lot in the last year or so. He's been a lot more open and a lot more relaxed in himself. He is a huge star and that must be difficult to deal with sometimes. But he is good at taking the mick out of himself for being what he is. Some of the things he comes up with do make you laugh. He can be really funny and he's good value. He's so quiet a lot of the time, then he says things and you can't believe he's said it. Gav is his own guy and he always has been.

A lot of people have strong opinions about him and he's come in for plenty of stick from various quarters. But, personally, I think he's great for the game. People speak about Jonah Lomu and what he did to increase the profile of the sport worldwide in the 1990s. Well, Gavin has done that for the Welsh game. He's just brought that something different and has got a lot of people interested in the game who perhaps wouldn't otherwise have been, particularly youngsters. After the Grand Slam, you would see loads of young kids with spiked-up Gavin hairstyles, and anybody who makes the next generation get involved in the game has to be applauded.

Not that it's just kids who have copied Gav. The scariest thing for me is that since he's come along, loads of the boys in the Welsh squad have started to shave their legs or go on sun-beds. I'm more one of the old school myself, so I stayed clear of that, but it just shows that he's brought that little bit extra to the game off the field. And he can also do it on the field. He's a phenomenal talent.

Personally, I think inside-centre is going to be his best position in the long run, because he gives you that extra dimension as a kicker, his defence is solid and he hits great angles in attack. Having him and Tom Shanklin in the centre during the Grand Slam was a really solid partnership and it was great to play off. Obviously Gav has had his problems with injuries since then and has had some tough times, but I hope he does have a future in the Welsh side, because he's a world-class player on his day and, as I say, he's good for the game.

It's easy to forget now, but there was a time when Iestyn Harris was just as much of a superstar in Welsh rugby. When he switched from rugby league in the autumn of 2001, it was a huge story and I was as excited as anyone by the news. I'd seen him playing for Leeds Rhinos quite a bit on television and I thought he was a brilliant player.

I really used to enjoy watching him, so I when I heard he was coming to Wales to play union and that he was joining Cardiff, it was just awesome. It was the biggest thing to happen to Welsh rugby for years.

The first time I met him, the thing I couldn't get over was how small he was. I just thought he'd be about 6ft and 15 stone, but he was really short. It shows how misleading watching games on television can be. But while he may not have been as big as I'd expected, there was no mistaking his talent, and that was obvious from his first start for Cardiff. It was a Heineken Cup game against Glasgow at the Arms Park in the October and he was chosen to play at fly-half. I was out injured at the time, so I watched on from the stand and, like everyone else there that day, I had my breath taken away by what I saw.

Iestyn was just sensational, scoring a hat-trick of tries in a 46–7 demolition of the Scots, and the whole of Wales went crazy. A lot had been made of the transfer fee the WRU had paid for him, but all that was now forgotten. Welsh rugby had found its new saviour. Everyone was euphoric. Wales had lost heavily at home to Ireland just a couple of weeks earlier and this seemed like the perfect tonic.

The only person who was a bit wary about it all was Iestyn himself. I remember him telling me that he went home to his wife Becky after the Glasgow game and said: 'That's the worst thing that could have possibly happened.' He knew it would just blow everything out of proportion and he was spot on.

The country went Iestyn-mad. Everyone had been

looking for the next big thing and here it was. A lot was expected of him, because he was a big name, but this was beyond anybody's wildest dreams. Nobody had ever seen a debut like it.

Unfortunately, everyone got a bit carried away, including the Wales coach at the time, Graham Henry. After Iestyn had played just two full games for Cardiff, Graham decided to throw him straight in at No. 10 for Wales' match against Argentina. It's unbelievable now to think they did that to him. There is not a player alive today that would have been good enough to cope with what he was asked to do.

When I got to know him better, he told me he never used to watch a lot of union before switching codes. It was all new to him and it's a totally different game to league. You've got to have played the game from a young age to understand what's going on and to able to read the game, especially if you are at fly-half. He'd never had ball off a line-out before, which he had to get used to, and when you are at No. 10 you are calling all the moves. If he had been a winger or a full-back, he might just have been able to get away with it, but not at fly-half.

But Neil Jenkins was coming towards the end of his career and people were looking for a new hero in the Welsh No. 10 jersey. So they turned to Iestyn.

I really felt for him in that game against Argentina. To chuck him straight in against the Pumas was asking the impossible. He was having to learn his rugby on the international stage and at No. 10 as well. That was absolutely crazy. You just can't do it. He ended up having a really tough time, conceding a charge-down try in a 30–16 home defeat and, in all probability, the whole experience set him back a long way.

He had been built up as the new Messiah of Welsh rugby and he was never going to be able to live up to the hype when he was such a novice in the game. You really need a good year to eighteen months to get to grips with union fully when you come from league, especially when you're playing in a pivotal position, and Iestyn was given just two games.

After that chastening experience against Argentina, he was moved to inside-centre for the next couple of internationals, but he was still being asked to run before he could walk and I know he found it tough.

As the months went by, I got to know him quite well and we became good friends, through being together with Cardiff and Wales. He's a good bloke and a really nice guy. His wife-to-be and my wife got really friendly as well and we went to his wedding at Miskin Manor, on the outskirts of Cardiff, in the summer of 2003. We had our photos in *Hello* magazine from that day and my missus is still happy with that. It's our claim to fame.

Iestyn was a really good pro, as you'd expect from someone who's come from league, but he would have his days where he'd be the grumpy northerner – and he wasn't exactly the most domesticated bloke either. In the World Cup in Australia in 2003, he was my room-mate when we were in apartments in Canberra and he was hopeless; he couldn't cook, he couldn't do anything.

But by then he could certainly do it on the field. The

season before that, he'd had some awesome games for Cardiff and he'd just started to shine for Wales at inside-centre.

With hindsight, twelve should have been his position in union from the start, not ten. It's ridiculous to come from league and play at ten. Henry Paul had the same problem when he tried to do it. It's like a quarterback in American football. You've really got to run the game and unless you've been doing that for a long time it's a big ask of anyone, I don't care who you are.

If he'd played in the centre from the start, it wouldn't have been so bad, because he was used to that second receiver's role from league and he would have found it easier to bed in there. But by the 2003 World Cup he was really looking the part at twelve and he had a good tournament. It had taken him a while to find his feet, but now he was really looking at home. And yet, just a few months later, he announced he was going back to league.

It's a shame that he left just as he was really kicking on and starting to make his mark. The longer he was here, the better he got and you could have seen a lot more out of Iestyn Harris in union.

If he'd stayed at twelve he would still be playing for Wales now and having a big impact on the side. But you can't really blame him for going back up north: he wanted to be closer to his family.

I still keep in touch with him now and I know he loves it up there. He obviously had a bit of stick because he joined Bradford, who are not best mates with Leeds, but he's doing his talking on the pitch. I've watched a few of his games over the last year or so and he's slotted straight back in like he'd never been away.

And I suppose the great irony is that by going back to league, Iestyn opened the door at twelve for the next Welsh rugby superstar, a certain Mr Henson.

## chapter 17

# ruddockgate revisited

It's the question I've been asked time and time again over the last year or so: 'What really happened with Mike Ruddock?'

Just about everyone I meet wants to know the inside story behind Mike's resignation as Wales coach midway through the 2006 Six Nations championship.

There have been no end of conspiracy theories doing the rounds and a lot of them have pointed the finger of blame at us as a group of players.

I obviously can't speak for Mike and it's not for me to explain his reasons for going, because only he can do that. But I do want to take this opportunity to put the record straight on behalf of the players, because I feel we've been unfairly vilified over the whole 'Ruddockgate' affair.

Mike was appointed national coach in succession to the homeward-bound Steve Hansen in the spring of 2004. It caught everyone by surprise because Gareth Jenkins was the public's favourite and we all thought he was going to get the job. Mike had withdrawn from the running a couple of months earlier, so it came as a big shock when he was unveiled.

There was a huge outcry at the time because people felt Gareth had been harshly treated by the Welsh Rugby Union, but it didn't really impact on me that much. I obviously knew both Gareth and Mike by reputation, but not on a personal or professional level, so I didn't have any particular feelings either way on which of them should get the job.

The big thing I wanted as a player was continuity. I felt it was vital that Scott Johnson, Andrew Hore and the defence coach Clive Griffiths stayed as part of the set-up, because we had put a lot of work in together and we all felt we were really getting somewhere. The one worry I had was that it was going to be a clean sweep. So I was really pleased when it was announced that they would be staying on under Mike, who was moving across from the Newport Gwent Dragons.

I'd played under him for Wales A when I was a lot younger, but only briefly. I'd never really worked with him on a day-to-day basis and I couldn't say I knew him. The first contact I had with him after he took over from Steve was when he rang me up just prior to the 2004 summer tour of Argentina to tell me I was being left behind. It was a strange call really. The way he worded it was not that I'd been dropped, but that he wanted me to stay behind to do conditioning work. That's how I took it anyway. But then, when I got off the phone, I thought: 'I've just been axed by him.' So that wasn't a great start.

Soon after that, I played in a testimonial match for Neil Jenkins at Sardis Road and I remember my old Pontypridd team-mate Richie Collins saying: 'Oh, he's given you that old chestnut has he,' when I told him what Ruddock had said. I don't know whether Richie was saying it in jest, but it sowed the seed of doubt in my mind that I wouldn't be involved under the new coach. I started thinking perhaps I wasn't in his plans and that he was just letting me down gently. It was at that point that I decided I was going to prove the guy wrong.

That summer I worked harder on my fitness and was more dedicated than I'd ever been before as regards to diet and looking after myself. I even trained during our family holiday to Sardinia. I was getting up at 6am in the morning to go for a five- or six-mile run along the beach and then in the afternoon I'd leave my wife and daughter to go to the gym. I really wanted to prove a point. Richie's words had really got to me.

Looking back, it was going to be difficult for whoever was coaching Wales at that time. We'd been through so much together as a group of players, getting knocked and slated, and we'd become so tight. We'd gone on a journey of discovery under Hansen and Johnson and come so far as a side. They were just constantly on your back, in terms of standards off the field and your own individual analysis. All of that was hammered home to you all the time. We'd had our eyes opened and been taken to a place we hadn't been before. So it was always going to be a hard job for a new coach to come into.

For me, the biggest thing Mike did was that he didn't try and change anything. He just let it be. He came in and just went: 'Right, Johnno, you're running the side, you're putting the gameplan and all the plays together, I'm not going to tinker with that because it's obviously working.'

That's to his credit, because a lot of coaches would have wanted to put their own stamp on things. Mike saw what we were doing was working, we were improving and he just kind of went along with that. So we carried on in pretty much the same vein as before and the 2005 Grand Slam was really the culmination of three years' work.

But even during that campaign there were issues with some players who didn't feel we were getting challenged like before. We had become used to being challenged every single day under the previous regime, challenged to improve and become better players. Now it felt as though that wasn't happening as much. There was a feeling Mike wasn't really bringing anything new to the party.

He didn't touch the backs, because Johnno was doing his stuff with them and, as a pack, he had us doing some very back-to-basics drills in training. But any kind of simmering discontent was covered up by the wins. It's like anything, when you are winning a lot of what's going on is covered up. So while there was a bit of an issue over Mike not challenging us, it never came to the surface because of the success on the field.

But while there had been enough momentum to carry us through that Grand Slam season, you have to look to move on again and we didn't do that. If anything, it felt as though we sat back and it didn't feel as though there was enough direction coming from the top.

So really, our 41–3 defeat at home to New Zealand the following autumn was an accident waiting to happen. We had the excuses of having a lot of players missing through injury and with boys having been on the Lions tour, but that match was a big wake-up call for us.

That autumn of 2005 was a difficult time for me, because I'd just lost my mother and the funeral was the Friday before the All Blacks game, so obviously I wasn't involved in that match. I remember watching it in the house and, just after the anthems finished, I had a text from Andrew Hore saying: 'Our thoughts are with you.' That was a great thing for him to do and it meant a hell of a lot to me.

When I went back into the Welsh camp the following week, I wouldn't say I wasn't really bothered about rugby, but I had bigger things on my mind. I was just going there and getting on with it and not really looking at things in too much depth.

But it was clear to me there had been rumblings and concerns that we'd gone into the comfort zone. Things had started to happen where Mike wasn't at sessions where we felt he needed to be. Or when he was at sessions he wasn't getting the best out of us.

Our next game was against Fiji, which was my first one back, and it was a game we almost lost. It was after that close shave that the rumblings about discontent in the camp first came to the surface in a couple of newspaper articles.

On the face of it, everything had been fine and dandy since Mike had come in to do the job. We'd had a great autumn in 2004 and a fantastic Six Nations in 2005 and there was no reason for anyone outside the camp to think anything was wrong. Unless you are involved in the scenario on a day-to-day basis you simply don't know what's going on.

But those games against New Zealand and Fiji were the first outward signs that things weren't quite so rosy in the Welsh rugby garden. And, as the autumn series went on, things seemed to be getting progressively worse.

We lost to South Africa and then, prior to the final match against Australia, we had the worst training week I've ever been involved with. We had one day down at the RAF base in St Athans where we were down there at 9am and didn't get home until 8pm. It was just such a badly organised day and the boys were really starting to get their backs up. I remember thinking we are never going to win this game, but it just goes to show you can't read too much into training weeks, because it's all about what happens on the Saturday. We beat the Wallabies in a thriller, to send Andrew Hore home to New Zealand on a winning note, and things were all hunky dory again … but not for long.

A couple of months later, we opened the defence of our Six Nations title against England at Twickenham and were soundly put in our place, being thumped 47–13.

After that, the murmurings started again and things quickly came to a head.

A lot of the English and Welsh boys had got friendly on the Lions tour to New Zealand the previous summer, so Matt Dawson had invited us to go to a VIP room at a London club after the game. It had all been agreed beforehand that we would go out. There was an eight-day turnaround until the next game against Scotland and we were told we could go. But then, because of the size of the defeat, Mike turned around and said he'd changed his mind.

That got the boys' backs up in itself: the worst thing, though, was that he didn't actually come out and tell us himself. The message was simply passed down the line and we finally discovered Mike didn't want us to go through Alfie. This was on the bus from Twickenham back to our hotel.

If Mike had just got up and explained why he didn't want us going out, it wouldn't have been so bad, but it never came out like that. That lost him a bit of the boys' respect.

As I understood it, he didn't want us going into the centre of London with the English boys because he thought there might be adverse press. Now our values as a squad up until that time were that we couldn't let outside influences dictate the way we act. Whatever happens, we've got to be in charge of ourselves. Once outside influences start dictating to you, that's when things start going wrong. All the players were disappointed, because we felt he was worrying too much about what other people thought rather than doing what was best for us as a group.

The way it's been reported in some places is that we ignored what he said and went out anyway. But that's not the case. He didn't want us to be seen in the middle of London; in the end a compromise was reached. There was a chat between the players and the management and it was agreed we'd go somewhere else, just as quiet, and that's what we eventually did.

Somehow, a version of that whole episode got into the press and a big issue was made of it. We weren't sure how that had happened and the atmosphere was a bit frosty when we got back into camp a couple of days later to prepare for the game against Scotland the following Sunday.

It was during the early part of that week that a group of us met up with Steve Lewis, the WRU chief executive, at our Vale of Glamorgan base. There was myself, Alfie, Stephen Jones and Brent Cockbain. We'd asked for the meeting as a squad to discuss insurance cover, following the serious shoulder injury suffered by Gareth Cooper in the England game. But, because things hadn't gone so well at Twickenham, Steve asked a few questions and just sort of said: 'What's going on boys?'

Now if you believe some of things you read, this is supposedly where we said Ruddock had to go. But that simply wasn't the case. We didn't say we wanted him out or that we thought he should go. What we did say was that we felt that perhaps we'd slipped back into old ways and gone back a few notches. Steve asked us the question and we were just being honest.

We also made it known that, whatever happened, from the players' point of view, we couldn't lose Scott Johnson. We had lost Hansen, we'd lost Hore, we just said whatever you do you've got to try and keep Johnno, because we felt that if we were going to keep on developing, we needed him there. We owed him so much and we were adamant that the WRU had to do everything in their power to try and keep hold of him.

People have read things into that and made out that we

were saying: 'You've got to get rid of Mike to keep Scott,' but that was never the case. Scott's issue was with his family and his kids back in Australia. I don't think in his heart of hearts he wanted to go. We just said to Steve to do whatever he could to try and keep him, even if it was a case of giving him six months in Australia and six months in Wales.

A lot has been made of that meeting, but there was no personal attack on Mike and it was never a case of us saying we wanted to get rid of him. It was just purely that we felt we'd let a lot of things slip. We were saying it not just from a coaching perspective but from the players' point of view as well.

We've also had the finger of blame pointed at us over the incident later that week where we backed up Alfie by boycotting a press conference, an episode which I described in the previous chapter. Some people have accused us of undermining Mike's authority by not following him into that conference, but the reason we weren't there didn't have anything to do with him, that was just an issue we, the players, had with one particular journalist.

The game against Scotland went ahead as normal at the Millennium Stadium that weekend and we got back on track by winning 28–18, with Alfie scoring two tries. We had no idea what was just around the corner.

On the face of it, the following Tuesday – St Valentine's Day – seemed just a normal training day. Mike had taken a session and there was no hint of anything out of the ordinary. But then, back at home that evening, I just remember hearing, the same as everybody else, that the WRU had called a press conference with immediate effect. I didn't have a clue what it was all about at first, but then I found out that Mike had resigned and after that my phone just went mad. It was red hot with calls and texts for the next couple of hours, with players ringing each other and friends and family trying to find out what was going on. It was a huge story. It was unheard of for a Wales coach to resign halfway through a championship. People were just saying: 'How could this happen?'

It didn't take long before you heard the first mention of 'player power' and that was to become just about the most-used phrase in Wales over the next few weeks. People had decided we had forced Mike out and there was no shaking them from that belief. That weekend, the *Wales on Sunday* newspaper had a picture of the Welsh team on the front page under the headline 'Accused'. You couldn't get much more pointed than that.

The rumours going about at that time were nobody's business. The one that riles us all the most is that we were supposedly jealous because Mike had been awarded the OBE and got all the credit for Grand Slam. Really petty little things like that started to emerge. Because it was such a shock and no one could believe what had happened, people started looking for deeper reasons and then started to make all these assumptions. It's just amazing how things can get perceived.

The finger of blame was also pointed at Johnno. Because he wasn't a Welshman, he was an easy target. People knew he was like a father figure to a lot of the boys and they put two and two together and came up with five, coming to the conclusion that he'd manipulated the whole situation. But Johnno wasn't involved in Mike's resignation in any way. He just kept doing what he did best, which was coaching. People are paid to give their opinions on things and that's up to them, but I think a lot of accusations were thrown without any real evidence.

I am still constantly being asked about it now and everyone seems to think that there was more to it than went on. Perhaps there might have been between the WRU and Mike, I just don't know, but as far as the players are concerned, we are as blind as anyone to what actually happened.

Prior to him going, I had never had any inkling that he might be unhappy. Afterwards, we heard rumours that he'd handed in his resignation after the New Zealand game in the autumn and that he hadn't been happy with it all for a while. But at the time, we didn't know anything about that and, come the Six Nations, we fully expected him to be there for the whole championship.

It's hard for me to say what Mike was thinking, but perhaps he might have sensed how close a lot of the players were with Johnno. It was always going to be a difficult place to come into, because we had become such a tight group together. He might have felt it was always going to be an uphill battle to try and gain respect the way that Scott and Steve had.

When you look back, there were probably signs along the way, with his new contract not being signed. That does show that perhaps things were not as rosy as everyone thought off the field. But I don't think we've got anything to reproach ourselves with as players. A lot of people have given us stick for going out after the England game and for not backing him at that press conference a few days later but, as I've said, I don't think people have been aware of the full story behind those incidents. And as for the rumour that we told Steve Lewis the WRU had to get rid of the coach, well that's just rubbish and I know because I was at that meeting.

I just think everything has been magnified and blown up out of all proportion because Mike resigned halfway through the Six Nations and less than a year after the Grand Slam.

I totally reject the idea that we forced him out. Yes, there were some issues, I'm not denying that. We felt there were certain sessions and certain times when he wasn't there, and when he was, we felt we weren't being challenged enough. Results hadn't gone that well and there were issues among the players because we didn't feel as though we were going forward. We'd stalled after the Grand Slam and, during that next season, we felt as though we were starting to go backwards.

But there are always going to be rumblings and things you think should be done better. That's happened in every squad I've ever been in. There's always going to be players unhappy with what's going on. It's just the nature of the game. How many people are always happy with their boss 24-7?

There will always be mini-revolts and questioning of the head coach. Things like that will go on in every team in every sport. You are not in a dictatorship. You have guys with a lot of opinions and those will always come to the surface.

I wouldn't say I was ever close to Mike. Some coaches

you develop a really good relationship with and you speak with them about things other than rugby, but I wouldn't speak to Mike about off-the-field stuff in the way I would with Johnno and Hansen.

But I have got no personal issue with him whatsoever. There's no bitterness against him from any of the boys as far as I know. Comments have been made that the players were jealous because Mike got so much attention, but that's absolute rubbish. The players had nothing against Mike whatsoever. He's a great guy. But we just felt we weren't getting challenged under him as we were before.

The issue a lot of us have is the way we were portrayed, as if it was us against Mike. That's how people have perceived what happened and it's just not right. There was never anything personal between Mike and the boys, far from it. But there was no changing people's views at the time.

That was despite the best efforts of Alfie in trying to stand up for the boys. I can still remember him ringing me up a couple of days after Ruddock had resigned to tell me he was going to be on the *Scrum V* programme on BBC Wales that Sunday. I asked him whether he was going on there with anyone, because I thought perhaps one of management would join him, but he just said: 'No, I'll go on there on my own.'

Feelings were obviously running high at the time because the day he went on TV there had been that 'Accused' headline in the papers following some poll which said it was our fault that the coach had gone. So, anyway, I sat down to watch the programme and the rest is history. I can just remember after about ten minutes the phone and the texts started going mad. People you hadn't heard of for years were saying: 'Have you seen Alfie on *Scrum V*?'

It all kicked off pretty much as soon as the programme started. The former Wales captain Eddie Butler and the show's presenter Gareth Lewis were grilling Alfie on the rumours that Ruddock had been forced out by player power and he wasn't about to take a backward step. It was just typical Alfie. There he was with his Motorhead T-shirt and leather jacket, getting more and more animated as the debate went on.

You couldn't really blame Butler and Lewis, they were just doing their job. It was the story of the day in Wales and they were trying to get to something. But like a lot of people, they were trying to dig further beyond what actually happened. Anyway, it ended up like car crash television.

Alfie took a lot of stick after that for the way he reacted during the interview, but a lot of things he said were spot on. I challenge anyone to be put in that position, if you're not trained to do it, and to do any better. He's a very emotional guy and I bet he doesn't regret a word of what he said. He said what he felt and that's always been his way.

After the show, he was taken ill and I know the whole episode over Ruddock affected him personally. He took a lot of it on his shoulders because he was captain and because he felt a responsibility to stand up for the boys.

He took all the flak for the squad, which is why the boys looked up to him the way they do. He could have easily dragged other people in there, but he fronted up like a good captain should and took the responsibility on. He's had more stick than anyone and he's been vilified over the whole affair, which I think is really wrong, but, despite his efforts, the stick kept coming.

I remember going to Ireland for our next championship game the following week, with Johnno as caretaker coach, and it seemed as though the whole world was against us.

That was a really difficult time and it just goes to show you never know what new crisis is around the corner in Welsh rugby. But I just hope with the passing of time that people can now start to see the whole Ruddockgate saga in a different light.

## chapter 18

# time to turn selector

It seemed a pretty straightforward task on the face of it. Choose two teams, a Wales XV and a World XV based on the best players I've played with and against during my career.

Little did I realise what I'd let myself in for. It's been a nightmare trying to finalise these two sides and it's reminded me just how many fantastically talented people I've been fortunate enough to share a rugby field with. But after many hours of soul-searching I've finally settled on my two line-ups, so here goes, starting with the Wales XV.

At full-back, it's Kevin Morgan, or 'The Rat' as everyone knows him. He is probably the player with the most nicknames in the Welsh side. He used to be known as 'Fluff' because of his attempts at a beard when he was younger, while Dwayne Peel calls him 'Keenan' after the Gareth Keenan character out of *The Office*. There is a lot of banter between those two over which one of them looks more like him. They both call each other Keenan, so it's whoever can get in first really. Kevin's also known as 'The Knife', or at least he'd like to be. He gave himself that nickname because he carves people up when he comes into the line! But 'The Rat' is the one. He got called that when he first turned up at Pontypridd, because he was so small and like a little rat scurrying around the place. It's stuck ever since.

For a guy who is so slight, Kev is as tough as they come. His defence for a small guy is unbelievable and he's as brave as anyone, while his attacking ability, with the angles he picks, is second to none. You would have seen so much more of him at international level if he hadn't had two career-threatening knee injuries. When the Celtic Warriors fell through in 2004, nobody wanted him initially because they thought he was finished, which is amazing for a player of that quality. He eventually went to the Dragons and proved everyone who had written him off wrong.

Gareth Thomas was always going to be in my team, it was just a question of where. I could have picked him anywhere from fifteen to eleven because he's such a talent and so versatile. I've put him on the right wing for the balance of the team as much as anything.

Obviously Ieuan Evans was a world-class player in that position, but I only really caught the end of his career and never played with him at his peak, so it's Alfie at fourteen.

Outside-centre was a really a difficult one. Mark Taylor was great for Wales, while Allan Bateman was one of my heroes when I was growing up. But, similar to the situation with Ieuan, I didn't play with Allan when he was at his very best, so I've gone for Tom Shanklin. When

Shanks is in the team the side has got a different dimension. He's got it all really. He's such a strong, powerful player, but not in the sense that that's all he can do. He's got great vision, good skill, good hands and his defence is outstanding. I've not seen many people dominate Brian O'Driscoll, but Shanks is one of those who has done just that.

When he first turned up with Wales, he was at Saracens at the time and no one really knew him. We just thought: 'Who's this public schoolboy nerd?' He looked like a bit of a geek for want of a nicer word. He had this posh accent – well posh by our standards – and it took a while to get to know him. But when we did, we realised he was a top bloke. The banter between Shanks, Kevin and Peely is one of the highlights of the squad. They are like the three stooges together. He's great fun Shanks, a really witty, sharp guy. He has got another side to him where he can be the moodiest so-and-so, but generally he's great to have about, off the field as well as on it.

There's no contest at inside-centre. It has to be Scott Gibbs. He was probably my favourite player when I was younger, so to end up in the same Wales team as him was a surreal experience. It was strange playing with him, because I was really in awe of the guy. He had such an aura about him and he was very much his own man off the field. At his peak, he was a phenomenal player and he's a shoo-in for me at twelve. He's one of the first names on the team-sheet.

He played for Wales when they weren't at their best, but he still came out of it as one of the greats. His reputation goes before him worldwide and not just in this country, especially because of what he did with the Lions in South Africa in 1997. He was such a tough guy and he did everything in the game.

On the left wing, it's Shane Williams. I would say, in terms of raw talent, he's the most naturally talented player in either team. You can't use enough superlatives for him. When you play touch rugby in training, it's not fair when he's not on your side. You should have an extra player on your team to make up for him. He's such a small guy, but he's a gutsy, tough little player as well, and the things he can do with his feet and the skills he's got are awesome. When he's on fire, there's no stopping him.

It amazes me that he spent so long out of the Welsh team. Perhaps the fact that he didn't have the upper-body strength he has now held him back. He has bulked up a hell of a lot over the last couple of years. Whenever you play against him at regional level, the biggest part of your gameplan is don't kick to Shane. You don't want to be caught in a one-on-one in open space with him. It's virtually impossible and he's skinned me many a time. Off the field he is really quiet, but I get on with him fine. He just gets on with things and goes, usually quite quickly, because he loves his fast cars.

At fly-half, it's a tough one between Neil Jenkins and Stephen Jones. They are very similar players. For tens, they are defensively very strong and very solid and they've both got brilliant rugby brains and can run the game. They are also great people off the pitch and really top blokes. So it's a difficult choice, but Stephen would probably have a go at me if I didn't pick Jenks in front of him, so Jenks it is.

Along with outside-centre, scrum-half was the hardest call. I've gone for Dwayne Peel over Rob Howley purely because of age; Dwayne has done everything younger. That is literally it. Both of them are world-class players and both could be said, at certain times of their careers, to be the best scrum-half in the world. They are very similar. Both are so sharp upstairs, they've both got the tap-and-go as their trademark and they both have the ability to do the right thing at the right time – just that rugby instinct. You can't coach a player that: they've either got it or they haven't. Rob was brilliant to me when I was coming through as a youngster in the Welsh squad and he's now my coach at Cardiff. So it's going to be extra training sessions for me when he sees I haven't picked him!

Like Rob, Dwayne is a model professional. He's totally dedicated to rugby and he's got a very old head on young shoulders. If I was advising a young player to model themselves on anyone at the moment I would say Peely, because he's such a good pro. He's great fun as well and has got a great sense of humour. He needs it at times, because he's a big Swansea City fan and he gets a fair bit of stick about that as there's a couple of Cardiff City boys in the squad.

Turning to the pack, loosehead was tricky to a certain degree because Duncan Jones is a great player but, for me, Gethin Jenkins is the best prop I've ever played with. He's got a freakish engine for a man of his size and he's got great skills. He's a good footballer and a really good scrummager as well. He's the whole package. Because he's such a big guy, people keep trying him at tighthead, but I think that takes away from what he is: a world-class loosehead.

Off the field, he just moans about everything. He's either moaning that we are training too hard or not training enough, or saying the food is no good. He does it so often now it's par for the course. Everyone just takes it with a pinch of salt. But he could moan for Wales. In fact, he would be captain if there was a Welsh moaning side. The boys just laugh about it now.

I've got to know him really well since he's come to Cardiff. 'The Melon', as he's known because of the shape of his head, is basically my training partner. Whenever we do extra sessions I always do stuff with him. All he does is sleep and train, but he's another one who's got a really dry sense of humour.

At hooker, Jonathan Humphreys was someone I had a huge amount of respect for. He was so good for me at Cardiff and you'd want to go into war with Humphs, he's that kind of player. He put his body on the line so often and was a great player. But I've gone for Garin Jenkins because a lot of what the 1999 Wales pack did was down to him. Peter Rogers and Ben Evans got a lot of praise for their scrummaging, especially after we went out to Argentina and won, but for me Garin was the cornerstone of that pack. For those couple of years under Graham Henry, he was the heart of the forward unit.

He was a real hard man, but a real funny guy as well. He was a great impersonator and he'd take off anyone, Henry included. I remember he stitched Arwel Thomas up one day by pretending to be Dougie Lawton, the old Widnes rugby league coach, and saying that they wanted

Arwel up there. He used to get on the mic at the front of the team bus and pretend to be a holiday rep. He was great at things like that, and really good value.

Dai Young was another real hard man on the field and you could see why he'd picked up the nickname 'The Enforcer'. He was such a big lump and a real presence on the tighthead.

I played with him after he came back from a long spell in rugby league. A lot of Welsh boys haven't got that much of a reputation or respect up north, but Dai is definitely an exception to that rule. I spoke to Barrie McDermott, the Great Britain prop, at Iestyn Harris' wedding and he said Dai was renowned in league as a hard man which, given the nature of that sport, is saying something. As a player, Dai did it all. Capped at nineteen, a Lion at twenty-one, then seven years in league and back to union to play international rugby again and captain his country.

In the second row, it's a tough one between Gareth Llewellyn and Brent Cockbain. Brent made a huge impact in a short space of time culminating in the part he played in the Grand Slam. He's exactly the sort of player you hate playing against. He's an absolute nightmare. He's all elbows and he hits rucks hard and does a lot of the dirty work people don't like doing.

But for Gareth to do what he did over that amount of years and still to be going now is phenomenol. He, more than anyone, benefited from Hansen, Hore and Johnson. He always looked after himself, but he got better still when they turned up and played his best rugby. He got better as he got older, without a shadow of a doubt.

Alongside him in the second row it's Chris Wyatt, the one-man riot. I went around the world with him playing sevens in the early part of my career, to places like Japan, Uruguay and Dubai, and he was a phenomenal sevens player. He was a great athlete; he had superb footballing skills and the biggest pair of hands you've ever seen in your life, like the foam hands football supporters have. There was no doubting his ability, but everyone was questioning whether he could do it internationally at fifteen-a-side. Well, for two years he was basically the only line-out option for Wales.

Looking back, he was a real enigma. He seemed to live on Coca-Cola, coffee and fags and he'd be up on the Playstation until three in the morning. But then he'd still go out and play awesomely on the Saturday. That's just how he got the best out of himself.

Maybe he could have achieved more and had a couple more seasons at international level but, on the other hand, I don't think he would have wanted to change anything. Off the field he was a great character. He loved life and he had a bit of the old school in him when it came to touring and things. But, at that time, he was a world-class second row.

Turning to my own little world in the back row, I'll start with Ryan Jones on the blind-side flank. Ryan, or 'Jug Head' as we call him, made a huge impact during the Grand Slam season, with the Scotland game being his real breakthrough match. Then when he went on the Lions tour and did what he did with so little experience showed how good a player he is and how good a player he's going to be. Everyone always points at his ball-carrying, but if you see his stats after games the amount of work he gets through is phenomenal, which is why I think he makes such a good six.

At seven, it's Colin Charvis. There are a lot of players who play in your position that you never really get on with, but Charvy and I have never been like that. I get on with him and we've never had cheap shots when we go on the field. It's probably because I've roomed with him a lot.

The press and public are sometimes not his No. 1 fans, but he's great among the boys. Everyone takes the mick out of his Brummie accent and of the fact that he falls asleep in meetings and things. But from a playing perspective he's absolute world class and someone I've got a huge amount of admiration for as a player. He was a great leader as skipper and a great senior player.

I think he's a bit misunderstood, because he's not your typical Welsh rugby player and very much his own man. Controversy has always seemed to follow him, whether it's his fault or not people can make up their own minds, but trouble never seems to be too far away as far as Col's concerned and I don't think he really minds.

Sometimes, though, it's gone over the top. After we lost to Italy out in Rome in 2003, he was voted the second most-hated man in Wales in some poll, in between Osama Bin Laden and Saddam Hussein. That was just ridiculous and it shows we take rugby just a bit too seriously in this country at times.

Last, but certainly not least, it's Scott Quinnell at No. 8. SQ *was* our gameplan under Graham Henry and he lived up to that role. But when I thought he was really awesome was in Australia with the 2001 Lions. I roomed with him for the last fortnight in Manly and he'd get up in the middle of the night and you'd hear his knees cracking and creaking. He'd be in agony. He'd limp to the toilet and you'd think there was no way he'd be able to make it on Saturday. But he went out there and was absolutely unbelievable. When we beat France out in Paris in 2001 he was awesome as well. I played against him a few times and he was a real handful. He's another one that went to league and anyone who does it in both codes deserves the utmost respect, because only a few have managed it. Off the field, he's a really good bloke and a big family man. He's very loud and bubbly, always upbeat. You see him when he's commentating on telly now and he's always bubbly and smiling.

Now for my World XV.

In my book, Chris Latham is the perfect full-back. Not that I thought so initially. I remember watching him on TV and thinking he didn't look that fast and was a bit awkward when he ran. But when you play against him you realise he's really quick, he can kick the ball a mile and he's as good as anyone under the high ball. He's a strong guy, a big bloke and his defence is rock solid.

It's another Aussie on the right wing in Lote Tuqiri. It might surprise people that I haven't gone for any of the current All Black fliers, like Sitiveni Sivivatu or Joe Rokocoko, but they play in an awesome side where you are always going to look good as a winger.

Tuqiri doesn't play in anything like such a stong side, but still really catches the eye, so that's why he gets the nod. I first played against him in 2003 in Australia and he made a big impression on me. He was just massive and quick with it as well. I've watched him in Tri-Nations matches and he's single-handedly kept Australia in a couple of games. The way he comes in off his wing can be devastating, while his defence is awesome.

I've gone for two Leinster players in the centre, one of them fairly obvious, the other, less so. Starting with the obvious: Brian O'Driscoll is someone I've got on well with during my two Lions tours and he's an absolutely unbelievable talent. He's like three or four players rolled into one. He's quick enough to be a winger, he's like an extra back-row player with the way he contests at the tackle area, he can kick a ball better than a lot of fly-halves and he's got all the attacking and defensive strengths you need in the centre. The guy has just got so much all-round talent and he's someone everyone in the game has a huge amount of respect for.

So who to partner him with at inside-centre? Aaron Mauger is a class player and so was Jeremy Guscott, whose career I just caught the end of, while the guy who I think is going to be the best twelve in the world is Luke McAllister, the young Kiwi. But, at this moment in time, I am a big admirer of Felipe Contepomi, of Leinster and Argentina. He's very similar to O'Driscoll in that he pinches ball at the tackle, he can kick well and he's just got great rugby instincts and so much flair about him. He's one of those players I'd pay to go and watch.

Someone who's probably put more bums on seats than anyone else during his career is my left wing, Jonah Lomu. I played for Wales A against him at Sardis Road in 1997, just a couple of years after he'd run over everyone at the 1995 World Cup, and it was a scary experience. No one had ever seen anything like him at the time. Here was this guy who was as big as a second row and as quick as any winger to have played the game. He was just a phenomenal athlete and he took the game to another level. He did a huge amount for the sport in terms of exposure and raising its profile.

I bounced off him twice in that A-game, but when I played against him for Wales in 2002 I somehow managed to tackle him twice. It's something I still wear as a badge of honour. He joined Cardiff Blues towards the end of 2006, which was a huge coup for the region. To be able to say you've played with Jonah Lomu is something in itself. He wasn't with us for long, but he was a real gentleman, a really good guy and very generous. There were just little things, such as the time when he bought a stereo and left it at the club for the boys in the changing room. He just had that touch of class about him.

Next up, it's the latest All Black superstar, Dan Carter. He's as good as I've ever seen at ten and, like all great sports men, he seems to have all the time in the world. He's so laid back and he's got the looks as well which helps, but he backs it up with his performances on the pitch. A lot of people might say it's easy behind that New Zealand pack, but I think he helps make that side.

Jonny Wilkinson is obviously another world-class fly-half and they are both match winners. But Carter has just got that extra gas and edges it in terms of attacking. There's no doubt he's something special.

I've come up against plenty of outstanding scrum-halves, including Joost van der Westhuizen and Justin Marshall, but George Gregan is the man who gets my vote. He's not a big guy, but as tough as they come and a really intelligent player. The first time I played against him, out in Australia in 2003, I can remember him shouting: 'Roll away, red seven, roll away.' That's what a ref does, so I automatically moved, but as I was rolling away, I realised it was Gregan. That's just typical of the Aussies. That's how sharp they are ... and Gregan's the sharpest of the lot.

Moving on to the pack, Sylvain Marconnet is someone I could have picked on either side of the front row, because he's world class in both positions and there are not many players you can say that about. He is an absolute monster, but it's not just his scrummaging. He's so mobile around the park as well. He's one top player.

Keith Wood was close at hooker but, for me, Keven Mealamu just does everything. When you analyse the All Blacks, you realise what a big role he plays. He does a lot of the dirty work, but he's also so strong with the ball in hand and he's really quick, with great feet as well. He's such a natural rugby player. There's a lot of stuff there that you just can't coach into someone.

Completing the front row is another Kiwi, Carl Hayman. Sometimes you see players on the telly and they look huge, but then when you play against them you realise they're not that big after all. But Hayman isn't one of those. He's just a man mountain. He could be a second row he's so big.

For people to say New Zealand's weakness lay in the front five when we went out there with the Lions was an absolute joke. Their scrum was huge and Haymans was the cornerstone of that pack. Speak to any of the top props and they'll say it's very difficult to work out a way to get the better of him.

If I was choosing a captain for this World XV it would have to be Martin Johnson. He was a great leader and his record speaks for itself. One of his best quotes was: 'A great team makes a great captain, but a great captain can't make a great team.'

He has always said that the likes of Lawrence Dallaglio, Will Greenwood and Matt Dawson did as much talking as he did in the England dressing room. And I remember with the Lions in 2001, Keith Wood would do a hell of a lot of talking. But that's what made Johnson such a good captain. When he did speak it wasn't a case of 'Here he goes again', but rather 'He's saying something, so it must be important'. When he spoke people definitely took notice. And he didn't say one thing and then not do it. He backed up his words with actions. He led by example and you didn't want to let him down.

As well as being a great captain, he was also a great second row in his own right. He was as hard as nails and an absolute pain to play against. If it was your line-out ball, he would climb all over the second row as they were winning it, and at rucks and mauls he was such a big guy that he was absolute nuisance value. But he was a talented rugby player as well, with his offloading and angles of running.

It's all about balance in the boilerhouse and I think Victor Matfield would provide the perfect partner for Johnson. South Africa have got one of the most efficient line-outs around and a lot of that is down to Matfield. He's a great technician and he dominates that area of the game. He loves to get the ball in his hands in open play as well and have a run. He tends to pop up all over the place. Back home, he's known jokingly as 'the best centre in South African rugby', which says a lot about the way he likes to play.

The biggest compliment I can give to George Smith is that he's as good as Richie McCaw. A lot of people will be surprised at that, but I'm a huge fan of the guy. I think his best position is seven, but I can't leave him or McCaw out, so I've put the two of them together, with Smith at six.

They are the two best flankers I've ever played against. I've faced the likes of Olivier Magne, Richard Hill, Neil Back and Lawrence Dallaglio, but those two are different gravy. Smith is much more of a footballer. His passing ability is awesome and he's got a good kicking game, which I like as a flanker.

But McCaw is just a freak, in the nicest possible way. He's not a big guy, in the sense of being muscle-bound, but he reads the game superbly and he's the ultimate seven in that he pushes the laws to the edge, and that's your job on the open-side.

His fitness and his intelligence are probably his two biggest assets. You get a lot of boys who are super fit, but when you see them running around they are a bit like headless chickens. But he's always in the right place at the right time. In the way that Michael Jones changed open-side play in the 1980s, McCaw has down the same now and brought a whole new dimension to the contact area: he's just streets ahead of everyone else and one of the main reasons why New Zealand are so good.

Another reason is Jerry Collins, who rounds off my World XV at No. 8. I can still vividly remember the first time I came across him, playing for Wales in Hamilton in 2003.

He hit me once and I'd never been hit like that before in my life, but I got off lightly compared to Colin Charvis. What he did to Charvy that day is something I'll never forget.

Charvy was a good ball-carrier, but Collins just lined him up and absolutely smashed him. Colin knew it was coming and was braced for it, but he still couldn't do anything about that and was knocked clean out. I was about five yards away from it and I still shudder at the thought.

People always talk about Collins' physicality, and understandably so, but he's got another side to his game which makes him such a dangerous player. A lot of people don't realise how good a footballer he is. He does a lot of little offloads and passes before contact. It's not just all ball under the arm and crashing through – although he can do that when he wants to as well.

So there you have it. Those are my two teams. I think the World XV would probably just have the edge, but it's a game I would love to watch. And when I think of all these fantastic players I've shared my career with, I realise just what a lucky man I've been.

| WALES XV | WORLD XV |
|---|---|
| 15. Kevin Morgan | 15. Chris Latham |
| 14. Gareth Thomas | 14. Lote Tuqiri |
| 13. Tom Shanklin | 13. Brian O'Driscoll |
| 12. Scott Gibbs | 12. Felipe Contepomi |
| 11. Shane Williams | 11. Jonah Lomu |
| 10. Neil Jenkins | 10. Dan Carter |
| 9. Dwayne Peel | 9. George Gregan |
| 1. Gethin Jenkins | 1. Sylvain Marconnet |
| 2. Garin Jenkins | 2. Keven Mealamu |
| 3. Dai Young | 3. Carl Hayman |
| 4. Gareth Llewellyn | 4. Martin Johnson |
| 5. Chris Wyatt | 5. Victor Matfield |
| 6. Ryan Jones | 6. George Smith |
| 7. Colin Charvis | 7. Richie McCaw |
| 8. Scott Quinnell | 8. Jerry Collins |

# career statistics

**Wales**

**1996**
Barbarians (Cardiff) Aug 24 W 31–10
France (Cardiff) Sept 25 L 33–40
Italy (Rome) Oct 5 W 31–22 [as replacement]

**1998**
Italy (Cardiff) Feb 7 W 23–20
England (Twickenham) Feb 21 L 26–60
Zimbabwe (Harare) June 6 W 49–11
South Africa (Wembley) Nov 14 L 20–28
Argentina (Llanelli) Nov 21 W 43–30

**1999**
Scotland (Edinburgh) Feb 6 L 20–33
Ireland (Wembley) Feb 20 L 23–29

Canada (Cardiff) Aug 21 W 33–19
Japan (Cardiff) Oct 9 W 64–15
Samoa (Cardiff) Oct 14 L 31–38

**2000**
England (Twickenham) March 4 L 12–46 [as
replacement]

**2001**
England (Cardiff) Feb 3 L 15–44
Scotland (Edinburgh) Feb 17 D 28–28
France (Paris) March 17 W 43–35
Italy (Rome) April 7 W 33–23

**2002**
Ireland (Dublin) Feb 3 L 10–54
France (Cardiff) Feb 16 L 33–37
Italy (Cardiff) March 2 W 44–20
England (Twickenham) March 23 L 10–50
Scotland (Cardiff) April 6 L 22–27
South Africa (Bloemfontein) June 8 L 19–34
South Africa (Cape Town) June 15 L 8–19
Fiji (Cardiff) Nov 9 W 58–14
Canada (Cardiff) Nov 16 W 32–21
New Zealand (Cardiff) Nov 23 L 17–43

**2003**
Italy (Rome) Feb 15 L 22–30
England (Cardiff) Feb 22 L 9–26
Scotland (Edinburgh) March 8 L 22–30 [captain]
Ireland (Cardiff) March 22 L 24–25 [1 try]

France (Paris) March 29 L 5–33 [captain]
Australia (Sydney) June 14 L 10–30 [captain]
New Zealand (Hamilton) June 21 L 3–55 [captain]
England (Cardiff) Aug 23 L 9–43
Canada (Melbourne) Oct 12 W 41–10
Tonga (Canberra) Oct 19 W 27–20 [1 try, 1 dg – as replacement]
Italy (Canberra) Oct 25 W 27–15
England (Brisbane) Nov 9 L 17–28 [1 try – as replacement]

## 2004
Scotland (Cardiff) Feb 14 W 23–10
Ireland (Dublin) Feb 21 L 15–36 [captain]
France (Cardiff) March 7 L 22–29 [1 try – as replacement]
England (Twickenham) March 20 L 21–31 [as replacement]
Italy (Cardiff) March 27 W 44–10
South Africa (Cardiff) Nov 6 L 36–38 [as replacement]
Romania (Cardiff) Nov 12 W 66–7 [as replacement]
New Zealand (Cardiff) Nov 20 L 25–26 [as replacement]
Japan (Cardiff) Nov 26 W 98–0 [as replacement]

## 2005
England (Cardiff) Feb 5 W 11–9
Italy (Rome) Feb 12 W 38–8 [1 try]
France (Paris) Feb 26 W 24–18 [2 tries]
Scotland (Edinburgh) March 13 W 46–22
Ireland (Cardiff) March 19 W 32–20

Fiji (Cardiff) Nov 11 W 11–10
South Africa (Cardiff) Nov 19 L 16–33
Australia (Cardiff) Nov 26 W 24–22

## 2006
England (Twickenham) Feb 4 L 13–47 [1 try]
Scotland (Cardiff) Feb 12 W 28–18
Ireland (Dublin) Feb 26 L 5–31
Italy (Cardiff) March 11 D 18–18
France (Cardiff) March 18 L 16–21
Australia (Cardiff) Nov 4 D 29–29 [1 try]
Canada (Cardiff) Nov 17 W 61–26
New Zealand (Cardiff) Nov 25 L 10–45 [1 try]

## 2007
Ireland (Cardiff) Feb 4 L 9–19
Scotland (Edinburgh) Feb 10 L 9–21
France (Paris) Feb 24 L 21–32
Italy (Rome) March 10 L 20–23
England (Cardiff) March 17 W 27–18
Argentina (Cardiff) Aug 18 W 27–20
France (Cardiff) Aug 26 L 34–7
Canada (Nantes) Sept 9 W 42–17
Australia (Cardiff) Sept 15 L 32–20
Japan (Cardiff) Sept 20 W 72–18 [2 tries]
Fiji (Nantes) Sept 29 L 38–34 [1 try]

## 2008
England (Twickenham) Feb 2 W 26-19
Scotland (Cardiff) Feb 9 W 30-15
Italy (Cardiff) Feb 23 W 47-8

Ireland (Dublin) March 8 W 16-12
France (Cardiff) March 15 W 29-12 [1 try]

Caps: 81 (W 38, L 40, D 3)
Points: 73 (14 tries, 1 dg)

## NON-CAP WALES GAMES

**1998**
Border (East London, SA) June 16 L 8–24
Natal (Durban) June 19 L 23–30

**1999**
Tucuman (Tucuman) June 1 W 69–44 [captain]
Argentina A (Rosario) June 8 L 34–47 [captain]
USA (Cardiff) Aug 30 W 53–24 [captain]

**2000**
French Barbarians (Cardiff) May 27 W 40–33

**2001**
Barbarians (Cardiff) May 20 L 38–40

**2002**
Barbarians (Cardiff) May 29 L 25–40

**2003**
Barbarians (Cardiff) May 31 L 35–48

## WALES A

**1997**
New Zealand (Pontypridd) Nov 11 L 8–51

**1998**
Scotland A (Newport) March 7 L 10–18
Ireland A (Limerick) March 20 W 42–27

**1999**
France A (Perigueux) March 5 W 20–17
Italy A (Rovigo) March 19 L 23–24
England A (Wrexham) April 9 W 32–25

**2000**
New Zealand A (Cardiff) Nov 10 L 9–30
South Africa (Cardiff) Nov 22 L 15–34

## BRITISH LIONS

**2001 Tour of Australia**
Queensland Presidents' XV (Townsville) June 12
W 83–6
Australia A (Gosford) June 19 L 25–28
NSW Country Cockatoos (Coffs Harbour) June 26
W 46–3
ACT Brumbies (Canberra) July 3 W 30–28

**2005 Tour of New Zealand**
Bay of Plenty (Rotorua) June 4 W 34–20

NZ Maoris (Hamilton) June 11 L 13–19
Otago (Dunedin) June 18 W 30–19
Southland (Invercargill) June 21 W 26–16
Manawatu (Palmerstone North) June 28 W 109–6
Auckland (Auckland) July 5 W 17–13 [1 try]
New Zealand (Auckland) July 9 L 19–38 [as
replacement]

## BARBARIANS

v East Midlands (Franklin's Gardens) March 11, 1998
W 50–40
v South Africa (Twickenham) Dec 1, 2007
W 22–5

## CLUB/REGIONAL CAREER

Pontypridd (1993–99)
Debut v Waterloo (Blundellsands) Oct 16, 1993 W 29–9
1993-94: Appearances 1 Tries 0 Points 0
1994-95: Appearances 2 Tries 0 Points 0
1995-96: Appearances 13 Tries 5 Points 25
1996-97: Appearances 24 Tries 6 Points 30
1997-98: Appearances 29 Tries 5 Points 25
1998-99: Appearances 30 Tries 8 Points 40

Total: Appearances 99 Tries 24 Points 120

Cardiff (1999–2003)
Debut v Swansea (St Helen's) Nov 13, 1999 W 34–25
1999–2000: Appearances 21 Tries 4 Points 20

2000–01: Appearances 24 Tries 2 Points 10
2001–02: Appearances 15 Tries 1 Points 5
2002–03: Appearances 20 Tries 5 Points 25 [captain]

**Cardiff Blues (2003–)**
2003–04: Appearances 12 Tries 2 Points 10  [captain]
2004–05: Appearances 16 Tries 2 Points 10  [captain]
2005–06: Appearances 19 Tries 4 Points 20
2006–07: Appearances 19 Tries 2 Points 10
2007–08: Appearances 15 Tries 4 Points 20

Statistics correct up to August 2008